Experimental Cinema

Experimental Cinema

David Curtis

A DELTA BOOK

A DELTA BOOK

Published by
Dell Publishing Co., Inc.
1 Dag Hammarskjold Plaza
New York, New York 10017

Originally published in the United States of America in 1971
by Universe Books and in Great Britain in 1971 by Studio Vista Limited

Delta ® TM 755118, Dell Publishing Co., Inc.
Reprinted by arrangement with Universe Books.
Printed in the United States of America
Third Printing

Acknowledgments

I am grateful to the following for supplying stills for reproduction: the National Film Archive, Steve Dwoskin, Ian Robertson, the London Film-makers' Co-operative, Vaughan Films, Twentieth Century-Fox, Paramount Pictures, the American Embassy (London), Bill Moritz and Progressive Art Production (Munich). Special thanks are due to the personal generosity of the film-makers themselves.

For assistance in the preparation of this book I should like to thank John Broderick, Regina Cornwell, Steve Dwoskin, Al Deval, Birgit Hein, Derek Hill, Erica Hunningher, Malcolm Le Grice, Jonas Mekas, Bill Moritz, Alan Sheperd, P. Adams Sitney, Albie Thoms, Jimmy Vaughan, Paul Willeman, the Information Department of the British Film Institute, the Lillie P. Bliss International Study Center (Museum of Modern Art) New York and the film-makers, too numerous to list here, whose correspondence and conversations provided the real substance of this book.

Contents

Experimental Cinema

The economic structure

Though still and movie photography originated from the same chemical discovery, their evolution during the nineteenth century led them to take almost completely opposed social and political roles. Still photography was dominated almost immediately by the amateur, serving in a collective capacity to record public news events, but basically acting as chronicler to the private individual, recording birth, graduation, marriage and death. Movie photography, on the other hand, served in this role for less than five years—the 'actuality' photographed by the Lumière brothers and their contemporaries was popular between 1895 and 1900, but its success was entirely dependent on the novelty of the medium. While the full resources of the still-photography industry were put behind developing cheap cameras for amateur use, in cinematography the early patent holders saw film's greatest potential as a theatrical art form, and did their best to centralize and limit production to an appropriate theatrical format. In 1909, Edison, Biograph, Vitagraph, Essanay, Selig, Lubin, Méliès and Klein (as the Motion Picture Patents Company) collectively tried to enforce the world-wide recognition of their sole licence on all movie production and exhibition equipment. Though this attempted monopoly failed, it stimulated the growth of large 'invulnerable' companies, which replaced the smaller independent production units and eventually led to the adoption of block booking and the circuit release of films through chains of cinemas. Perhaps the relative expense of movie making made this kind of development inevitable, though the combined camera/printer/projector used by Lumière's cameramen suggested at least one alternative line of development.

The film entertainment industry that emerged between the wars was based on the craft and ingenuity of the studio technician. Technical innovations, such as sound and wide-screen systems, required considerable capital investment and might never have been contemplated without the security afforded by centralization and the tight control of exhibition outlets. Films were made on an unprecedented scale—returns on investment being virtually guaranteed.

As the cinema became popular it rapidly assumed a powerful role as arbiter of public taste and morals. Both Lenin and Pope

Pius XI recognized its potential strength: 'There exists today no means of influencing the masses more potent than the cinema' (Pius XI). 'The cinema must and shall become the foremost cultural weapon of the proletariat' (Lenin). Feature directors still justify their work by the moral stand they have taken; few make any claims to have explored the camera's ability to emulate and enhance human visual perception—the unbiased use of the eye and the complex visual judgments of the mind. The true amateur is often freer to experiment in this field than the so-called professional. Consequently some of the best work has been made by independent film-makers, working consciously as film-artists, outside the 'industry'.

The USA led the world in terms of film production between the wars, but severely lagged behind in all but technical experiment. American dominance of world markets forced Europe into recognizing the political and 'educational' relevance of the motion picture almost before the Americans themselves. Worried by the anti-German message in American movies, the Germans took the unprecedented step of nationalizing their film industry in the hope of restoring a national cultural identity. Italy, whose film industry had thrived before the war, followed suit as soon as Mussolini came to power. Lenin nationalized the Russian cinema in 1919 and centralized all production in 1924. Nationalization became the pattern for all European film-production and has significantly remained so for radio and television broadcasting. The advantages were the same as those sought by the Motion Picture Patents Company—the strength of monopoly and the centralization of capital resources, with the further doubtful advantage of allowing direct government intervention to protect the public interest.

Yet, initially at least, the nationalized industries seemed to stimulate artistic achievement. The first years of UFA (Universum Film AG—the German national studios) gave Lang, Murnau, Pabst and their fellow directors the surroundings and equipment with which they produced their finest work; Russian centralization was immediately followed by the most creative work of Eisenstein, Pudovkin and Kuleshov. UFA in particular were quick to emphasize the cultural and aesthetic excellence of their product, and to their credit were the first major studios to support the work of individual film-artists—Richter, Eggeling and Ruttmann—though their generosity did not extend to the exhibition of their works.

Richter and Eggeling, however, were not the first graphic artists to become involved with the cinema. In Italy the Futurist movement produced at least two films by painters, Aldo Modinari's

Mondo Baldoria (1914)—of which Marinetti strongly disapproved—and A. G. Bragaglia's *Perfido Incanto* (1916) starring Marinetti, Balla and Chiti among Futurist sets. Marinetti's Futurist Manifesto, which was full of pronouncements on the cinema, was well known internationally, but it is doubtful if either film was ever seen outside Italy.

The European avant-garde

FRANCE 1919–30

It was in France, where there was no nationalized industry, that the pattern of independent experimental production first evolved, if only temporarily, as a structure separate from the commercial cinema. As in America, the French had 'rationalized' film distribution and exhibition, though production remained largely in the hands of independent studios.

The first world war, which temporarily halted all production, was followed by a period in which many of the smaller companies capitulated to the expanding American movie empire. However, a number of vocal minority groups began to make themselves heard at this time. Initially these men were critics, not directors, and they established a precedent for the movement from criticism to direction followed by Godard, Truffaut, Chabrol, etc.

The Italian, Ricotto Canudo, did much to popularize a serious interest in the cinema through his columns in *Les Nouvelles Littéraires*. More important historically was the appearance in January 1920 of *Cine Club*, a magazine created by Louis Delluc, which concentrated on establishing a respect for the 'cinematic' in movies, 'their ability to create beauty by movement and by editing, out of subjects not necessarily photographically beautiful in themselves'.[1]

Delluc's writing is as impulsive in its approach as his one true successor's—Jonas Mekas (see page 134). Neither disguises the passion in his judgment, in the belief that passion can inspire a real love and respect for the cinema. Like Mekas, Delluc did not limit his activities to journalism—in June 1920 he organized two conferences at the Pepinière Cinema in Paris: the first on André Antoine who shared Delluc's hostility for the theatrical (as represented by the Film d'Art series of stage play adaptations) and a concern for 'cinematic' mise-en-scènes; the second on Emile Cohl, the pioneer animator.

Soon afterwards, Canudo created the world's first film club—his Club des Amis du Septième Art (CASA), held first at the annual Salon D'Automne and then in a series of smaller Paris cinemas.

[1] Louis Delluc *Photogénie*, printed originally by Editions de Brunoff, Paris (c. 1919); extracts reprinted in Marcel Lapierre's *Anthologie du Cinéma*. Paris: La Nouvelle Edition 1946.

Neither Canudo nor Delluc felt at this time any need to differentiate between 'experimental' and 'commercial' cinema—they championed and exhibited the best of both. In France neither category was especially privileged in terms of production—capital and equipment were equally scarce to both, and by no means could all sections of the commercial cinema be sure of distribution.

In May 1921 Delluc launched a second magazine *Cinéa* which became the chief vehicle of his philosophy; and in the same year he was responsible for importing *The Cabinet of Dr Caligari*, which had just been a smash hit on Broadway. He then began to make films; of the numerous screenplays he wrote, he directed the best three himself: *Fièvre* (1921), *La Femme de Nulle Part* (1922) and *L'Innondation* (1924). They now appear to be within the best naturalistic tradition of the French cinema—all three making use of simple sets and particularly evocative locations. *Fièvre* and *La Femme* describe a nostalgia for the past (for a past love and for a vanished way of life), but their unsentimental and direct visual style marks a break with the melodramatic treatment characteristic of the period.

Neither Delluc nor Canudo lived long enough to see the full effect of their work—Canudo died in 1923, Delluc a year later, aged thirty-three. But Delluc in particular had already prepared for his successors. Jean Epstein, Marcel L'Herbier and Germaine Dulac, all involved in the running of *Ciné Club* and *Cinéa* at one time or another, continued to make experimental films and to encourage independent film screenings. Jean Tedesco, another collaborator, started his own full-time avant-garde cinema at the Théâtre du Vieux Colombier in 1924, directly acknowledging his debt to Delluc.

Following the French example, 'cine clubs' were opened in England, Holland, Germany and Switzerland. In England the Film Society was formed in 1925—its members including Ivor Montagu (the zoologist and later translator of Eisenstein), directors Adrian Brunel, Alberto Cavalcanti and Thorold Dickinson and a number of literary figures. In addition to introducing films from France, Germany, Russia and America, the society presented programmes on the technical aspects of film-making. Lecture/demonstrations were given by Eisenstein, Pudovkin and other celebrities. (Hans Richter conducted an abortive class in film-production held in studios rented above Foyles in Manette Street.) An important part of the society's policy was to fight the capricious and erratic censorship of the day.

The Anglo-French critic Jacques Brunius (collaborator on Luis Buñuel's *L'Age d'Or*) has suggested that the cine clubs had a distinct effect on the avant-garde film:

Romantic and expressionistic German films (*Caligari*, *Nosferatu*) stimulated a research into composition; American so-called comics, that ought rather to be qualified as poetic or lyric (Mack Sennett, Charlie Chaplin, Hal Roach, Al St John, Larry Semon, Buster Keaton, Harry Langdon) prompted a reconsideration of logic and reason; Swedish films (especially *La Charrette Fantôme*) released a wave of dreams and superimpositions, and later Soviet films (*Potemkin*) added fresh fuel to the preoccupation with cutting and editing.

Marcel L'Herbier, Jean Epstein and Germaine Dulac had formed part of Louis Delluc's critical circle (between 1919 and 1921); from that association stems the most consistent line of development in the French avant-garde movement. Marcel L'Herbier started to make films immediately after the first world war, but his first important work was *L'Homme du Large* (1920), a translation of a Balzac story set in Brittany that made effective use of the scale of the landscape. The following year—1921—the year of Delluc's *Fièvre*—he made *El Dorado*, a 'romantic anecdote' about a dancer Sybilla (played by Eve Francis) who sacrifices everything for the sake of her child. The story in fact accounts for very little in the film, providing an excuse for the figure of Sybilla to be seen in the open Andalusian landscape, which L'Herbier shot through filters in a conscious attempt to emulate the paintings of Riberra, Velasquez and Goya. In a sequence set in the Alhambra, the dancer's grief is conveyed by 'subjective shots of distorted architectural detail'.

The artistic side of L'Herbier reached its peak in *L'Inhumaine* (1923), in which Eve Francis competes with the extraordinary 'abstract' sets designed by Fernand Léger and Cavalcanti (plate 3). Brunius was contemptuous:

> L'Herbier thought he was being revolutionary in dressing and making-up his actors as for the Russian ballet, and putting them into pseudo-cubist decors or flimsy looking modern interiors made by Mallet-Stevens [the architect]. He withdrew from reality without ever succeeding in creating another emotion or building a poetic universe . . . The utter lack of imagination, sensibility or emotion, the sexual irresolution in directing the actors, the artificiality and *nouveau-riche* determination to be 'modern' at any price, reduces this experiment to a mere cerebral reaction of aesthetes.[1]

Ironically, the extreme 'artificiality' that Brunius objects to is exactly what people appreciate in the film today. In an interview

[1] 'Rise and decline of an avant-garde' *Penguin Film Review* no 5, 1948.

with Richard Roud (*Sight and Sound*, Summer 1969), Alain Resnais drew attention to another side of L'Herbier's work, his use of the popular novel—*le feuilleton*—as a vehicle for 'the subconscious, the surrealistic association of ideas [which are] present in the *feuilleton*—more than in other forms of art'.

After *L'Inhumaine*, L'Herbier levelled his sights towards the commercial cinema; his *Feu Mathias Pascal* (1925), a Pirandello adaptation, is famous for the performance of the Russian actor/director Mozhukhin, and Cavalcanti's sets—well within the range of public taste this time.

In *L'Argent* (1928), a Zola adaptation starring Brigitte Helm, L'Herbier made use of Gance's invention the 'portatif'—a suspended camera capable of moving and taking shots automatically without an operator—making possible 360-degree pans at very close quarters, spectacular 'flights' up staircases, etc.

Close to realizing Delluc's ideal were the first films of Jean Epstein. Coming from the world of literature, his first work was a commissioned documentary to commemorate the centenary of Louis Pasteur in 1922, but the same year he made a short version of Balzac's *L'Auberge Rouge*—using in the climax the accelerated cutting techniques introduced by Gance in *La Roue* (plate 6). In 1923 he made his masterpiece *Cœur Fidèle*. Somewhat in the style of Delluc's *Fièvre*, the story concerns the rivalry of two men —an 'honest worker' and a 'layabout'—for the same woman. It is set in a country town celebrating a wine festival. The film's attraction lies not so much in the virtuosity of the camera work (in one sequence the camera 'takes part' in the festivities) as in its sympathetic recording of the background to the conflict—drunken village life. Because of the subsequent over-use of the 'provincial idyll' by later French directors (and Epstein himself for that matter) it is difficult to imagine this scene without prejudice, but in its context it succeeds completely.

After *La Belle Nivernaise* (1924), as with L'Herbier, public taste more than kept pace with Epstein's creative achievement. He began to use exaggerated camera angles and rapid cutting almost arbitrarily, without direct reference to the story-line. At the end of the decade he made three films—*Six et Demi Onze*, *La Glace à Trois Faces* and *La Chute de la Maison Usher* (*The Fall of the House of Usher* 1928)—especially for art-house audiences. The last of the three is probably his best-known work but lacks the visual integrity of the American version by Watson and Webber of the same year. *La Glace* is interesting for its *Rashomon*-like narration of the story from four viewpoints. As if aware of a decline in his work, Epstein quite suddenly returned to making documentaries.

Dimitri Kirsanov, Russian born, worked in complete isolation from the avant-garde movement. He had come to Paris in 1919 to study the 'cello, but was inspired by Swedish films to make *L'Ironie du Destin* (1922–3), which has not survived. *Ménilmontant* (1924), however, still exists and is an extraordinary achievement. The film opens with a violent axe murder, shown in a succession of fragmented images lasting less than one minute (plate 4). Shots of the murderer, his hands, his arms dealing the blows; the murder weapon, striking, swinging again, dropping; the faces of the man and woman attacked, horror struck, falling lifeless, are intercut in an original and intuitive montage, which owes nothing to the Russian achievements of the same year, e.g. *Strike*, *Potemkin*, etc. The story develops to show the blighting effect of the murder on the girl and her sister as they grow up. It is told with an economy rare in the silent film: whenever possible the action is telescoped to indicate only the essentials—travel is represented by a rapid montage of car movement—in a series of dissolves the girls move from foreground to mid-shot to long-shot as they walk down an avenue. The camera cranes up to bring the lovers from street level to the bedroom. Successively increasing close-ups are used to intensify the emotion of the young girl as she discovers the bodies of her parents (plate 4)—a device hailed as a 'formal discovery' of the Russians (e.g. the close-ups of Alexandra Khokhlova in Kuleshov's *By the Law*). Kirsanov used it only once where it happened to be appropriate to the situation.

Ménilmontant was premièred at Le Vieux Colombier and enjoyed immediate popular success. Tedesco hailed Kirsanov's star Nadia Sibirskaïa as a 'new Lilian Gish'. The following year Kirsanov made *Brumes d'Automne* (*Autumn Mists*), a romantic cine-poem very much more subdued in style, again starring Sibirskaïa—this time as a woman alone with her thoughts (a theme taken up by Steve Dwoskin forty years later). The images are extremely beautiful, photographically—mists, the surface of water, falling leaves (a metaphor of the falling ashes of the letter Sibirskaïa burns), a complete landscape reflected in a muddy pool. In only one sequence Kirsanov allows himself to use a distorting lens to represent the tear-stained vision of his heroine.

The film is a masterpiece of its genre and by reputation alone has influenced many films, for instance, Herman Weinberg's *Autumn Fire* (1931). Kirsanov's first sound film, *Rapt* (1933), was the last film over which he had anything like complete artistic control. He himself did not consider any of his subsequent works to be worthy of attention—they included a number of commissioned short subjects and a 'well-made thriller' *Morte Moisson* made in 1949. He died in 1957.

Jean Renoir has been quoted as saying, 'My early work does

not, in my opinion, offer anything of interest. It has only one value, the interpretation of her roles by Catherine Hessling [Auguste Renoir's ex-model and Jean Renoir's wife], who was a fantastic actress.' Although it was not until the early thirties that he developed the committed humanist philosophy that distinguished his pre-war work, Renoir is perhaps too critical—at least two of his first films severely challenged conventional narrative structure.

Nana (1926) is generally accepted as being Renoir's major silent work. It features Catherine Hessling as Nana and Werner Krauss (Dr Caligari in the German film) as Count Muffat. P. Adams Sitney points out the film's 'exceptional formal rigor' and suggests that the contemporary revolution in literary fiction—Proust, Joyce, Stein, Virginia Woolf—might in some measure at least be responsible:

> What does this filmed version of a Zola novel share with the most avant-garde fiction of its day? Simply a sensual involvement with the fact of narrative. Before the 1920s a novel was synonomous with its plot, likewise a film (with few exceptions). In Renoir's film Zola's plot is incidental. It was the matrix within which the structure of the film is formed. In one of the film's finest incidents, the horse race, whose winner is crucial in any consideration of the plot, Renoir simply shows the horses hooves beating the turf. There is no individualization of horses, nor a change of running pace to suggest the beginning or end of the race. Just the hooves and the turf, intercut again and again with the character-spectators. An abstraction of this order would have been remarkable even if the outcome of the race made no difference to the situation; as it is, it marks a critical moment in the evolution of the fiction film. The horse race sequence is not the only significant abstraction in the narrative of *Nana*. Early in the film there is a unit of pure cinema, in which two men pass in opposite directions, oblivious to each other, and leave the shot empty. One is returning to Nana, the other is leaving her. The presence of this short shot, completely unnecessary to the plot, yet demonstrative of the interaction between narrative and space in cinema, proves the remarkable sensitivity of Renoir at this time, to the sensual presence of narrative.[1]

In his adaptation of the Hans Anderson Story *La Petite Marchande d'Allumettes* (*The Little Match Girl* 1928) Renoir came

[1] *Changes* magazine, New York 1969.

close to making an avant-garde film *per se*. Financing it himself, he consciously cut himself off from any likelihood of commercial distribution by making it for and in Le Vieux Colombier. Tedesco gave him a loft above the theatre, a car engine and a dynamo to power his lights. With models and dramatic lighting (as in the German studios), Renoir constructed the fantasy world inhabited by Karen, the matchseller, as she is dying. He added complexity to the story by making Karen both child and woman: she dreams of toys and of the handsome officer, who flying through the clouds on his horse comes, as the figure of death, to 'rescue' her. The film intentionally confuses the real with the imaginary, the images grow into each other, only the figure of Karen remains constant. 'Reality' is only certain when the girl's body is revealed at the end, covered with real snow in a real landscape.

To achieve the grey-scale values he wanted in the fantasy sequences, Renoir used the new panchromatic film, normally reserved for exterior work. To make this possible he constructed his own lights and developed each section of film himself in a neighbour's kitchen. To Renoir *La Petite Marchande d'Allumettes* was above all a 'technical exercise'. The film's public appearance was eclipsed, he recalls, by the arrival of the sound film.

Abel Gance would never have considered himself an avant-garde film-maker, but his technical innovations—the use of rapid cutting and of multiple images—demonstate his confidence in the public's acceptance of unusual visual experiments. In *La Folie du Docteur Tube* (1915), for example, a story about a hallucinatory drug, almost half the film is shot through a distorting lens (plate 5); but it is in *La Roue* (1923) and *Napoléon, Vu Par Abel Gance* (1927) that he displays his inventiveness to its greatest advantage. Kevin Brownlow, in *The Parade's Gone By*, cites an example of Gance's mastery of rapid cutting in *La Roue* (plate 6):

> The death of Elie . . . could not be cut faster. Gance starts by intercutting three frames of Elie's horrified face as he begins to lose his hold on the cliff's edge, with six of Norma. The speed increases to three of Norma and two of Elie, until a frenetic climax is reached, one frame of Elie, screaming, intercut with one frame of Norma. The sequence is given final punctuation of three frames of Elie taken from a different set, before we see his hand slip and his body fall.

> The sequence of rapid cutting in which Sifif is reliving the crash was written in the script [he quotes Gance]:
> 'On the original scenario I wrote: image 1—ten frames, image 2 —nine frames, image 3—eight frames and so on right down to

one frame. I thought that the eye would be quicker than the brain—that it would transmit to the brain the messages of the images. I didn't intend to startle; it just seemed the right way to do it!'

Despite the precalculation, this is not the psychological (Pavlovian) version of the Russian editing in which foreign elements are combined to elicit a predetermined reaction. Gance's cutting is 'impressionistic', designed to simulate the rapid intake of visual stimuli (as in a moment of crisis), or simply to present a visual metaphor.

Gance's most memorable early use of Polyvision (multiple screens) occurs in *La Roue* in nine separate sections, orchestrated together to work both as a visual whole and individually as subjective viewpoints in the battle. Later in the same film, in his famous cinerama effect, the screen triples its size, three projectors being used, sometimes with close-ups of the action to left and right, often the left mirroring the right, and sometimes extending the central action in one continuous (and synchronous) panorama; finally the screens were coloured red, white and blue 'and over this tricolour, I superimposed a huge eagle! The audience was on its feet at the end, cheering.' This was in 1927—*Napoléon* was premièred and ran complete in eight European capitals that year, before MGM bought it and cut it down to size.

By 1927, however, the European avant-garde was already developed and beyond Gance's influence. Nor does any connexion seem to exist between his innovations in France and the apparent affirmation of his pioneer work in the frequent use of the multi-screen and rapid cutting techniques in the American experimental film today, for he was and still is largely unknown in the USA.

The French avant-garde film is often taken to be the same as the Surrealist film—a tribute, perhaps, to the potency of the Surrealist Manifesto but a belief that gives a very misleading impression of the scope of French film-making in the twenties. Those writing about the period have tended to impose a number of differing categories and divisions; but none fits perfectly—the movement is too fragmentary to accept simple classification.

To add to the confusion, many film-makers changed course several times during the twenties. René Clair, maker of the key Dada work *Entr'acte*, was also responsible for two Expressionist fantasies *Paris qui dort* or *Le Rayon Invisible* (*The Crazy Ray*) and *Le Voyage Imaginaire*, and later the bourgeois comedy *Le Chapeau de Paille d'Italie* (*The Italian Straw Hat*) for which he was to become famous. Germaine Dulac, who made the first

Surrealist film as such *La Coquille et le Clergyman* (*The Seashell and the Clergyman*) revealed a sentimental side in her earlier *La Souriante Madame Beudet* (*The Smiling Madame Beudet*); she then made *Rhythme et Variations* which almost parodies avant-garde sensibilities.

Pure Surrealism, as projected by André Breton, carried forward the anti-art, anti-bourgeois, anti-war commitment of the earlier Dada movement, with its emphasis on chance and absurdity and its confrontation with 'the object'. To these it added a respect and an abuse of Freudian thought-association and a process 'automatism'—best defined by Breton himself:

> Surrealism. *n.masc.* pure psychic automatism, by which an attempt is made to express, either verbally, in writing or in any other matter, the true functioning of thought. The dictation of thought, in the absence of all control by reason, excluding any aesthetic or moral preoccupation . . .
>
> Surrealism rests on the belief in the higher reality of certain hitherto neglected forms of association, in the omnipotence of the dream, in the disinterested play of thought.[1]

Some Dada artists had shown an interest in cinema even before the first world war. Apollinaire, for example, had said, 'The great theatre which produces total drama is the cinema.' As a group, however, they showed little intention of becoming involved in the process of film-making until well after the French cine clubs had established the validity of the artist/film-maker's position.

Thereafter, both Dada and Surrealism made a powerful impact on the cinema, recognizing 'the unit of cinema' (Sitney's phrase) in its own right. Breton apparently visited local cinemas, 'in the hope of catching some bizarre chance happening recorded on screen in an American Western or serial'. Such bizarre chance happenings were to become the subject of their films.

René Clair, as a young journalist, took small parts in several French episode films, notably in Feuillade's *Parisette* in 1920. After serving an apprenticeship as assistant to Jacques de Baroncelli, at the age of 25, and on a very small budget, he started to make his first film—*Paris qui dort* (1923). Its plot is very close in feeling to the less believable side of the episode movie. A group of tourists on top of the Eiffel Tower, descend to find that the whole of Paris beneath has been 'stopped in time' by a mysterious ray. Seeking its source, the eight visitors see the city's inhabitants frozen, often in comic positions—for instance a pickpocket caught in the act. They prevail upon the mad professor responsible to start life moving again; at first he does so only half successfully—

[1] Maurice Nadeau *The History of Surrealism*. London: Jonathan Cape, 1968.

everybody moves in fits and starts. In fact the film is little more than an excuse for exploiting freeze-frame, slow and fast motion techniques, but as a comedy it works within these terms.

The next year (1924) Clair directed the first successful collective film of the avant-garde—*Entr'acte* (meaning 'intermission'); his collaborators were Picabia (scenario), Erik Satie (music[1]), Man Ray, Inge Fiis, Marcel Duchamp, Georges Auric, Jean Borlin and Erik Satie (actors). Rolf de Maré (producer) was responsible for commissioning the film as a piece to be projected during the interval in the ballet *Relâche*.

Also by Picabia, *Relâche* was performed at the Théâtre des Champs Elysées by the Swedish Ballet. The audience, or what remained after confronting the ballet's title (meaning 'performance cancelled'), were illuminated during part of the performance by a battery of projectors shining at them from the stage (anticipating some John Cage/Merce Cunningham pieces). The film itself presents, Dada-style, a series of objects and situations which bear little narrative relation—chance juxtaposition and direct visual association being used as the main source of comedy. A dancer is seen in a series of close-ups—her hands above her head, her legs as seen from ground level, looking like a multi-petalled flower, from directly beneath (filmed in slow motion through a sheet of glass). *She* is revealed to be a bearded man. Cigarettes form themselves into an orderly row and become the Parthenon. An egg stays suspended in a jet of water. Marcel Duchamp and Man Ray play chess on an open roof—their board becomes the Place de la Concorde. Events repeat themselves with the annoying and irrational frequency of a dream. In the famous funeral sequence a hearse drawn by a camel runs out of control down a hill; the mourners are seen first in comic slow motion, then at ever increasing speed—the chaotic procession involving everything in its wake. This, the last section of the film (a text-book example of skilfully constructed montage), is successful as a piece of comedy, but weakens the integrity of the Dada statement. The 'stray impulse', the essential motivator in the Dada construction of 'extreme contradictions', is sacrificed to a more traditional form—the Keystone chase.

Clair's humour and fantasy, as he demonstrates again in the delightful *Le Voyage Imaginaire* (1926), is too immediately sympathetic to fit the Dada/Surrealist aesthetic. In his prolific

[1] Satie's music no longer survives and there is an alternative version suggesting that Picabia had hoped to use the 'interval murmur of the theatre audience as a background noise for this [silent] film, but they all fell silent, as though the sight of [Clair's] extraordinary cortege had taken their breath away. Picabia, enraged, shouted at the audience, "Talk, can't you, talk!" Nobody did.' Hans Richter *Dada, Art and Anti-Art*. London: Thames and Hudson, 1965.

writing that dates from the mid-twenties, Clair suggests a much colder, more analytic sensibility than he was ever to show in his films: 'Let us return to the birth of the cinema: "The cinematograph, says the dictionary, is a machine designed to project animated pictures on a screen." The Art that comes from such an instrument must be an art of *Vision* and of *movement*.'[1] He implies the rigorous, automatic approach to film-making adopted by Léger, Man Ray and Duchamp. After 1925 Clair concentrated on making films for the commercial cinema.

Like other artists who turned to film-making, Man Ray, expatriate American painter and photographer, made films explicitly as part of his artistic output—none were intended for any kind of commercial exploitation. As well as bringing new ideas, these film artists also contributed techniques that gave the film a completely new appearance; Man Ray brought with him his animated 'rayogram'[2] which allowed the direct registration of objects on to film by physically placing them on the photographic surface and exposing them to light. His first solo attempt (he had collaborated with Duchamp on an unsuccessful experiment in three dimensions, see page 19) was a three-minute film called *Le Retour à la Raison*. It was made partly with the rayogram, using nails, springs, etc., intercut with shots of his Dada mobiles and strips of film with nude torsos printed on them (which in projection appear as a kind of superimposition). It was put together to be shown at the 'Soirée du cœur à barbe' (Evening of the bearded heart), with music by Auric, Milhaud and Stravinsky, films by Hans Richter, and poetry and plays by Tristan Tzara and others. Breton's violent interruptions made this one of Dada's last and most chaotic gatherings.

His next film *Emak Bakia* (1926; plate 7) was made, according to Ray, in strict conformity with Surrealist principles. It opens with a series of apparently unrelated shots: grain on film; flowers moving; drawing pins in negative; points of light—out of focus—which order themselves into lines; a signwriter spelling out incomplete sentences; a prism, reflecting bars of light, rotating at different speeds; car headlights, with a huge single eye superimposed over the radiator between them; it blinks; and so on. As the film progresses the car theme becomes dominant: the driver wearing goggles (which mimic the car's headlights). There follow a series of conventional shots of the car driving down an avenue, intercut with close-ups of sheep (in complete tonal contrast). The car stops—a woman's legs are seen getting out—the shot is

[1] René Clair 'Le cinema contre l'esprit' (1927) in *Anthologie du Cinema*. Paris: La Nouvelle Edition, 1946.

[2] His name for the process he discovered in still photography 1920–1.

repeated three times, the fourth time it fades and is replaced by a stepped superimposition of all four shots, one following closely on the other. Individual images are striking for their humour and originality, but Ray still apparently felt it necessary to impose a conventionally readable theme—the car ride—to hold the film together.

L'Etoile de Mer (1928; plate 8) is a more integrated and consciously 'surrealistic' work. Inspired by Robert Desnos' poem, a love affair thematically unites the whole film. The images are more obviously linked by (sexual) association: a collapsing factory chimney; starfish tentacles; a newspaper blowing in the wind; the view from a speeding train; a montage of a liner nudging its dock; its funnels; New York's foggy skyline. Recurring shots show the woman naked on a bed (through frosted glass) and the film's central metaphor—the starfish. Desnos' poem appears as a series of interrupting ironic titles.

Les Mystères du Chateau de Dé (1929) reverts to the anecdotal. Man Ray and J. A. Boiffard explore an art connoisseur's 'modern' chateau and construct a number of visual jokes around it. Strips of film are shown backwards and in negative; people play strange games on the lawn, kicking around two giant dice in an allusion to 'chance procedures'; the film is measured by disorientating shots of an empty landscape.

Ray's works contain neither the rigid sequential structure of the narrative film, nor the schematic/rhythmic form of the pure abstract artists (Léger, Eggeling, Richter) but their informality indicates the start of a new attitude to film-making in which the artist is free to reveal as much of the creative process as he chooses. This in turn demands of the audience a more responsible (less manipulated) kind of involvement with the images on the screen.

Following directly upon Man Ray's 'abstracted' light play sequences, Henri Chomette, René Clair's brother, made two short films using the same technique—*Reflets de Lumière et de Vitesse* (1925) and *Cinq Minutes de Cinéma Pur* (1926). Many others were to take up a similar form of exploration, Moholy-Nagy after leaving the Bauhaus made a series *Lightspeile* (1928–32), the English/Belgian team Blakeston and Brugière made their *Light Rhythms* in 1930, and in America James Davis made his *Light Reflections and Shadows* in 1948. These experiments have been largely superseded today by the 'live' form—the light show.

Fernand Léger made only one film, *Le Ballet Mécanique* (1924), the first completely abstract film to be *photographed* (as opposed to the drawn abstractions of Richter and Eggeling). Léger's objects flash on to the screen with no logic to order them; there is no theme, and if any thought-associations link them they are certainly not the obvious ones of Man Ray's *Etoile de Mer*. The *Ballet* begins: a woman smiling to herself, swinging, in mid-shot; two frames of a straw hat are followed by one frame of a clock face; two frames of three bottles are followed by two frames of the bottles in a different configuration; thirty-six frames of the straw hat are followed by 110 frames of a smiling mouth (followed by forty frames of the hat again). The film was made to be projected at 16–20 frames per second, so the clock, the first appearance of the straw hat and the bottles are almost subliminal.

Léger lit his objects with highly contrasting light and shadow, to 'reveal their personality', and this, together with his bursts of short cuts, results in an unusually animated screen. What was black immediately becomes white—the tonal match that is maintained throughout a conventional movie sequence is wilfully (joyfully) destroyed (almost in anticipation of Paul Sharits, page 157). His adherence to Cubism (he associated himself with neither Dada nor Surrealism) can be seen in his angular fragmentation and multiplication of images (saucepan lids, bits of typography) and his play on the pure circle and triangle (alternating, two frames each). In one quite extraordinary part of the film, he shows a large woman with a load on her shoulder (plate 9) climbing up a flight of steps. She is shown seven steps from the top; she climbs four and a half more, then suddenly she is back at the seventh again. Léger repeats her action, loopwise, ten times creating an abstraction of a movement/duration (an 'action' would not imply the dual awareness created) that probably ranks as the first completely conscious recognition of the 'unit of cinema' to be recorded on film. At last, film has become the subject of film.

Marcel Duchamp, another contemporary painter, whose interests and influence have ranged over almost every branch of artistic activity, showed surprisingly little interest in the cinema *per se*. His complete works in this field consist of an abandoned film, variously dated 1920 and 1923, and the completed *Anemic Cinema* (1926). Both were logical extensions of his study of optical phenomena. In his book, *Dada, Art and Anti-Art*, Hans Richter gives Man Ray's account of the earlier film, an experiment in stereoscopy:

> In 1920, Marcel and I made a film test about forty feet long, with two synchronized cameras, in order to photograph the same object [a sphere with spirals painted on it] from a slightly different position. This forty-foot test we decided to develop by hand. In order to do this Marcel prepared a tray with a wooden

> bottom into which he nailed about four hundred nails spaced at an equal distance. The tray was then filled with film developer and the film was wound round these four hundred nails, to be bathed and developed just like any photographic film. But in this process the film, that is the emulsion, stuck together and could not be disentangled. It was therefore completely lost, with the exception of a few frames.

Duchamp continues:

> The solution of this artistic problem finally came with *Discs* (1925) in which true three-dimensionality was achieved, not with a complicated machine (for example, the *Glass Machine* of 1920) or a complicated technique, but in the eyes of the onlooker, by a psycho-physiological process.

The first of these discs was made for the *Rotary Demi-Sphere* (*Precision Optics*) (1925), a motorized optical device; then seven others were drawn and together they form the visual material of *Anemic Cinema*. Each disc is a series of concentric, sometimes eccentric rings, and can be interpreted as it spins either as leading into the screen or out towards the viewer (plate 10). Between them there appear eight puns, written on a spiral and rotated to read, for example, 'Esquivons les ecchymoses des esquimaux aux mots esquis.'

Both the discs, expanded to become a series of twelve *Rotoreliefs* in 1935, and the verbal puns (on their discs) have been exhibited as artworks in their own right—a do-it-yourself movie kit in effect.

Toby Mussman has recorded (in *Film Culture* 41) that when *Anemic Cinema* was initially shown, Duchamp constructed a special projection screen of translucent glass, like that used in bathroom windows, with a mirror-silvered backing to gain an overall unstable, stroboscopic lighting effect. Though there seems to be no other mention of this, it certainly seems in keeping with the artist's approach.

In 1928, four years after Léger's *Le Ballet Mécanique*, Eugene Deslaw made his *Marche des Machines*. Though both were inspired by an appreciation of the mechanical, there is very little visual link between them. Deslaw's film requires the viewer to enjoy the film through empathy with the machines; he shows pipes, gear-wheels, conveyor-belts, always at a distance and with no particular rhythm. His one concession to continuity is to prepare the end of some shots for the beginning of the next—a shot of a wheel is masked to prepare for a shot looking down the interior of a boiler.

Only occasionally does the image become abstracted enough to make it enjoyable in itself, or explicit enough for the object to reveal its function. In all, it is a frustrating film. Deslaw's *La Nuit Electrique* (1930) was one of the first of many films to be made using illuminated street signs as its sole subject.

Germaine Dulac began her association with the cinema during the first world war, and included among her assignments a popular episode film *Ames de Fous* (1917). In 1919 she made the first of the films to star Eve Francis—*La Fête Espagnol*. The film had a Spanish setting, which Delluc's cinéastes felt had strong affinities with the Wild West; its scenario was by Delluc himself. But only with *La Souriante Madame Beudet* (1922) did she consciously adopt the avant-garde aesthetic. In this film she very literally illustrates the fantasies and inner frustrations of a romantic middle-aged woman who feels neglected and abused by her insensitive husband. The woman is sitting at her piano playing Debussy—the screen dissolves into a mass of sparkling highlights (photographed off water). When her husband sings opera to himself, costumed actors depict the various roles. As Madame Beudet reads a magazine, an advertisement for a tennis racquet sparks off a fantasy in which a handsome young player leaps from the pages in slow motion and carries off her husband (rather inaccurately suggesting his replacement in her affections). Later she sees him beat the piano in fast motion displaying his anger. Unfortunately the trick photography creates such clichéd situations that they can only seem comic today.

This same oversimplified pictorial conception detracts from Dulac's most famous film *La Coquille et le Clergyman* (*The Seashell and the Clergyman* 1926–7), an equally literal translation of an infinitely superior scenario written by Antonin Artaud. Artaud, who is probably best remembered today as the originator of the Theatre of Cruelty, was very much involved in the cinema. He acted parts in two major movies in the late twenties—Marat in Gance's *Napoléon* and Brother Massieu in Carl Dreyer's *La Passion de Jeanne d'Arc*—and according to reports very much wanted to play the clergyman in Dulac's film.

Historically Artaud's scenario is of great importance. Nothing could be less like the innocent fantasies dreamed up by René Clair or the 'pure' films of Léger and Richter. Artaud deliberately delved into the 'ugly' depths of the subconscious, and allowed his plot to embrace the full extent of the chaos he found there. An extract from the scenario of *The Seashell* which he published shortly after the release of the film gives an idea of his intention. The main protagonists are the clergyman, an officer and a young woman. The clergyman is in a ballroom and had just been confronted by a woman's ghost:

> The apparition seems to terrify the clergyman. He lets the breast-plate fall and it gives off an enormous flame in breaking. Then, as if he were seized by a feeling of sudden bashfulness, he gathers his clothes to him. But as he grasps the skirts of his cassock to draw them around his thighs, these skirt-tails seem to stretch out, forming an endless road into the night. The clergyman and the woman run desperately through the night.
>
> This race is interspaced with hallucinatory sequences with the woman in different guises: now with her cheek prodigiously swollen, now with her tongue sticking out, stretching out infinitely, with the clergyman hanging on to it like a rope. At times her breasts are grotesquely distended. At the end of the race the clergyman emerges in a passageway with the woman swinging in a sort of cloud behind him. We suddenly see a great iron-studded door . . .

The images have no narrative meaning, they are rather a series of visual stimuli intended to create a psychological drama within the viewer, 'rousing the mind by osmosis without verbal transposition'.

Dulac's cinematic 'transposition' is not always helpful. Her sense of pictorial design and too-well-measured editing (visual rhythm) detract from the essential realism of Artaud's vision. When the film was premièred at the Ursulines Club, Artaud apparently denounced Dulac's production and was supported in his attack by his Surrealist friends; but the circumstances suggest that this may have been more in anger at his exclusion from the cutting rooms than through any basic disagreement over the visual conception, as has sometimes been suggested.

Artaud wrote one further screenplay *The Revolt of the Butcher* in 1930 in which, 'eroticism, savagery, blood lust, a thirst for violence, an obsession with horror, collapse of moral values, social hypocrisy, lies, perjury, sadism, depravity, etc. have been made as explicit as possible'.[1] It was never realized. In its written form it appears to be even more powerful and anarchic than Buñuel's much acclaimed *L'Age d'Or* (*The Age of Gold*).

Dulac's later films—*Disque 927*, *Arabesque* and *Thème et Variation* (1927–30)—were visual interpretations of pieces of music. Resnais records (*Sight and Sound*, summer 1969): 'Her attempt to apply musical time to pictorial time was a real disaster.

[1] Artaud's introduction to *The Revolt of the Butcher*. Paris: Nouvelle Revue Française, June 1930.

(Mind you I'm glad she tried it, somebody had to.) Her mistake was in confusing aural and visual perception and retention.' Between 1930 and 1940 she directed the newsreel series *Pathé Journal*.

In 1927, the Spanish painter, Luis Buñuel, arrived in Paris to make films. He served a brief apprenticeship with Jean Epstein, working on *The Fall of the House of Usher*; in 1928, collaborating with his countryman Salvador Dali, he wrote and directed the classic Surrealist film *Un Chien Andalou*:

> Historically, this film represents a violent reaction against what was at that time called 'avant-garde cine', which was directed exclusively to the artistic sensibility and to the reason of the spectator, with its play of light and shadow, its photographic effects, its preoccupation with rhythmic montage and technical research, and at times in the direction of the display of a perfectly conventional and reasonable mood. To this avant-garde cinema group belonged Ruttmann, Cavalcanti, Man Ray, Dziga Vertov, René Clair, Dulac, Ivens, etc.
>
> In *Un Chien Andalou*, the cinema maker takes his place for the first time on a purely poetical–moral plane. (Take 'moral' in the sense of what governs dreams or parasympathetic compulsions.) In the working out of the plot, every idea of a rational, aesthetic or other preoccupation with technical matters was rejected as irrelevant. The result is a film deliberately anti-plastic, anti-artistic, considered by traditional canons. The plot is the result of a CONSCIOUS *psychic automatism*, and, to that extent, it does not attempt to recount a dream, although it profits by a mechanism analogous to that of dreams.
>
> The sources from which the film draws inspiration are those of poetry, freed from the ballast of reason and tradition. Its aim is to provoke in the spectator instinctive reactions of attraction and of repulsion. (Experience has demonstrated that this objective was fully attained.)

In 1929 Buñuel published the scenario of *Un Chien Andalou*: the opening sequence establishes the mood:

> 'Once upon a time.' A balcony at night. A man, Buñuel, sharpens his razor near the balcony; looks at the sky through the window and sees . . . a light cloud floating towards the full moon. The head of a young girl with large eyes. The light cloud passes in

front of the moon. The razor blade passes through the girl's eye, cutting it in two.

Buñuel's and Dali's approach to film-making differs radically from previous avant-garde works, especially in comparison with Dulac's *The Seashell and the Clergyman*. Dulac's work abounds in trick photography (for example, the woman's many metamorphoses during the 'race') and literal interpretations of Surrealist distortion of time and location. She uses the camera's technical resources to make visible (by masking, superimposition, etc.) the transition between one state and another. Buñuel, on the other hand, respects every convention of the narrative film, from its use of explanatory close-ups and locating long-shots, to its deliberate avoidance of 'artistic techniques'. He treats his subject as though he were making a popular thriller, presenting just enough 'continuity' and 'theme'—the pleasant bourgeois heroine, the recurring striped box, the physiognomical resemblance between the various men (are they the same man?)—to reinforce the illusion of rationality. This strengthens the impact of the extraordinary plot. It is the very innocence of the opening sequence, the man, the balcony, the romantic moon, that makes his irrational act—slicing the eye —so appalling.

Un Chien Andalou was enormously successful. Buñuel had hoped to avoid misinterpretation and denounced 'the crazy madness which finds beauty or poetry in this film, which is ultimately, nor more nor less than a despairing call to murder'.

His next film *L'Age d'Or* (1930) was made without Dali's collaboration. Surrealist images persist but in tone the film is closer to pure spiritual (and political) anarchy. It begins as a straightforward documentary on the life and habits of the scorpion —apparently harmless—but the size of the beasts is already menacing. To demonstrate their hidden venom, they are seen attacking each other and then killing a rat. The destructive tone of the film is thus established and quite suddenly the subject changes to a group of blind and crippled bandits (led by Max Ernst), armed with the useless tools of art, living in extreme poverty and squalor, defending their island against the invading 'Majorcans'. They die off one by one. A group of bishops stand chanting upon a rock (outmoded objects); they are later seen as skeletons, but continue to chant none the less. A boatload of bureaucrats arrives to lay the foundations of the *Age of Gold*— their ceremony is interrupted by a couple nearby, who, fully dressed, energetically make love in a bed of mud. This couple, and their attempt to consummate their love, becomes the central theme of the film. At every turn they are frustrated by bourgeois society: the couple are separated; the man is dragged off by policemen, who (in a sudden change of location) lead him through the streets of 'Imperial Rome'. Only by demonstrating his conformity (he reveals the right papers), is he able to regain his freedom and get back to the girl. The same papers admit him to a reception at her parents' house, where once again they attempt to make love. This time it is his 'conscience' that separates them, then the intrusion of her father. The man ends up in total frustration—he is forced to reject everything but in his rage there is at last a measure of freedom. Buñuel is in no doubt as to where the responsibility lies for his predicament.

In a final tableau, four debauched characters are seen to emerge from de Sade's Château de Selliny; a title tells us that they have just survived the '120 days of Sodom'; a Christ-like figure re-enters the castle to rape/kill a young girl—this is the depth to which Christianity has reduced human emotion. The meaningless violence of this last act is paralleled throughout the film: by the callous indifference of the bourgeoisie to the fate of their servants in a burning kitchen (during the reception); by the father who shoots his son for interfering with the lighting of his pipe. It has in turn contaminated the hero: as he is dragged from the girl, he viciously kicks at a dog that barks at them; running for a taxi he deliberately knocks down a blind man who gets in his way. Violence is both the problem and, by implication, the solution.

With his third film *Las Hurdes* (*Terre sans Pain* 1932)—a savage documentary on the appalling conditions suffered by the Honduras in north-east Spain—Buñuel demonstrated his complete break with the avant-garde.

L'Age d'Or marked the culmination of the whole avant-garde movement, which after 1930 had virtually ceased to exist—the reasons being both political and economic. It was becoming increasingly apparent that the rising social and political unrest in Europe (as manifest in the General Strikes in England and the rise of the Nazi party in Germany) was bound to lead to a major upheaval. With the rise of fascism, 'abstract' artists became the focus of repeated attacks. Many left for the safety of America. What initiative remained passed from the cine-club amateurs to those working in the popular cinema. Film-artists (Man Ray, Léger, Duchamp) gave way to directors (Vigo, Pagnol, Renoir, and later Carné).

The decline of the avant-garde was paralleled by the closure of France's major studios—independent producers stepped in to fill the void, making money available to Vigo for his *Zéro de Conduite* (1932) and *L'Atalante* (1934), and Renoir for his *Boudu* (1932),

Toni (1935), *Les Bas Fonds* (1936), *La Grande Illusion* (1937), etc. In these films in particular, artistic experiment was contained, in favour of more readily accessible social authenticity, in the valid hope that this would enhance their political impact. In Renoir's case, this was a conscious decision (paralleled by Jean-Luc Godard's professed position in recent years). This containment was of necessity complimented by a radical re-evaluation of the narrative film's dependence on the conventional storyline; at last the bourgeois melodrama could be replaced by a more honest confrontation of real social problems.

As a sequel to the avant-garde, Jean Cocteau—painter, poet, author and playwright—began his career in films in 1930 with *Le Sang d'un Poète* (*The Blood of a Poet*), which is often described as a Surrealist film. Cocteau certainly shared some of the imagery used by Dulac and Buñuel and has suggested the film's mood was 'a kind of half-sleep through which I wandered as though in a labyrinth', adding, however, that it 'draws nothing from either dreams or symbols'. *Le Sang d'un Poète*, financed by the Comte de Noailles (as was Buñuel's *L'Age d'Or*), was produced entirely as a professional undertaking: Cocteau hired a studio from Gaumont and employed Michel Arnaud as technical director and the celebrated Georges Perinal as cameraman. His own enigmatic commentary was supported by Georges Auric's music score.

The film traces the 'adventures' of a poet who 'lives out his own creations' in his mind (plate 12). A mouth he has drawn attaches itself to the palm of his hand; he transfers it to a statue which slowly comes to life (plate 13); it leads him through a mirror (the first of several such mirrors to feature in Cocteau's work) into the Hôtel des Folies Dramatiques. There he observes a series of tableaux vivantes representing the mysteries and enigmas the poet must face. The film incorporates a great number of special effects. Sets were constructed at an angle to allow a girl to 'fly' across a room and to follow the strange progress of the poet along the corridor of the hotel (he was filmed 'walking' while lying sideways on the floor, the camera mounted vertically above him). Mattes and superimpositions locate the moving human mouth in a plaster statue, then bring the whole statue to life.

Despite the film's numerous visual transformations and the deliberate disruption of the integrity of time and location, the overall effect stresses the film's continuity. Cocteau deliberately directed the audience's attention back to the central enigma of the poet's existence—a theme he returned to in his two films based on the Orpheus legend—*Orphée* (1950) and *Le Testament d'Orphée* (1959). Despite a prolific output in the intervening years, it was only in the latter, his last work, that he felt able to 'go beyond the plot'. In the films made during the intervening years, such as *La Belle et la Bête, L'Aigle à Deux Têtes* and *Les Parents Terribles*, he felt obliged to contain his visual inventiveness within a much more conventional narrative structure.

GERMANY 1919–30

At least three years before Man Ray and Fernand Léger created their abstract films in Paris, Hans Richter and the Swedish painter, Viking Eggeling, had made a similar breakthrough (with what Richter called 'absolute' films) in pre-war Germany. Despite Richter's involvement in the Dada movement, as film-makers both he and Eggeling worked in almost complete isolation. At no time during Eggeling's lifetime (he died in 1925) was there a regular screening place for his kind of film in Germany, while in France a complete 'alternative' cinema, with its own theatres, audience and critics, had already been established. Consequently, their contribution to the international avant-garde was not apparent until well into the mid-twenties.

In 1918 Richter and Eggeling began a long association in which they studied the principles of 'rhythm in painting'. Working together they completed a series of abstract drawings (variations on a theme) through which they hoped to reveal all the possible permutations of a number of basic relationships. From the confusion that resulted, they decided to fix the most successful drawings into a specific 'logical and convincing' order, which led to the idea of *Scroll* paintings—each scroll containing about twelve 'characteristic transformations'. From there it was only a short, but inspired, step to film.

Richter records that they were both daunted by the idea of using the 'mechanized technique of photography', but in 1920 he managed to persuade UFA to set their animators to work on his thirty-foot scroll *Prelude*. The laboriousness of the animators' technique discouraged them even more, but rather than abandon the new medium, Richter simplified his design to shapes more easily manipulated under the camera—cut-out paper squares. These he made in all sizes and in every shade from grey to white, making them 'grow and disappear, jump and slide in well controlled tempi and in a planned rhythm'. He called the piece *Film is Rhythm* and/or *Rhythmus 21* (*21* being the year in which it was made); it was 100 feet long and lasted for just over one minute. It was shown only once in this form, by Theo van Doesburg at the Théâtre Michel in Paris.

Eggeling, unlike Richter, was unwilling to modify his compositions to simplify their transition to film. Between 1920 and 1922 he laboriously completed the thousands of drawings necessary to animate his second scroll work, *Diagonal Symphony* (plate 14), completely redesigning it three times in the process. The *Diagonal Symphony* is an intensely beautiful work. Eggeling's line drawings (white on black) of wing shapes and harp-like forms grow and mutate, sometimes two shapes in counterpoint to each other, sometimes one alone turning on its axis, each figure lasting only for a few seconds (curiously similar to Robert Breer's computer-drawn figures in *69*, made some forty years later). *Diagonal Symphony* was shown briefly in Berlin in 1922, but Eggeling received no income from it. He died three years later, unable to make another film.

In 1925 the first international avant-garde film show was held in Berlin at UFA's theatre Kurfürstendamm. Films shown included Clair's *Entr'acte*, Léger's *Ballet Mécanique* and Eggeling's *Diagonal Symphony*. Hans Richter presented his *Rhythmus 23*, which incorporated parts of *Rhythmus 21* with new footage of diagonal bars that 'fill-up' and contract, parallel lines in harp shapes (an unconscious tribute to Eggeling) and a film-in-miniature (almost like computer digits) that appears from time to time in a corner of the frame.

The international show provided a great morale boost to German film-makers. 'The existence of *Entr'acte* and *Ballet Mécanique* proved to us that we belonged to something,' wrote Richter. In *Rhythmus 25* Richter painted the lines and squares by hand, using colour to 'strengthen' their expression. His films were beginning to become known in Germany and he started to receive commissions. Albertini, an acrobat, requested a 'trade mark in motion', Stella Simon, the American film-maker, asked for '100 feet of abstract waves' for use in her film *Hands* (released without Richter's footage in 1928). To help fulfil these projects, Richter built himself an animation rostrum, using a bicycle pump to regulate the shutter speed—an arrangement adopted later by both Berthold Bartosch and Alexandre Alexeieff (see page 34). On it he made *Film Study* (1926) a free association of abstract and figurative shapes: amorphous clouds; a 'sun' rises through them; a row of identical faces floating in a black field; eyes (pingpong balls with false eyes and lashes glued to them) rotating in space; a play of circles; a play of more 'realistic' eyes (plate 15); circles again; eyes multiplied; the faces superimposed; squares; a negative close-up of a mallet hitting the ground; moving spiral (of cigarettes?); a rock crowded with birds. The screen flashes from positive to negative, from negative to positive, the images linked by a flowing rhythm that makes the transitions seem quite natural.

Richter maintains that *Film Study* was 'one of the first Surrealistic studies developing from one sequence to the other by associations and analogies', but this was certainly not the Surrealistic association of Dulac or Dali.

In the same year he was commissioned by UFA to make an introduction for the film *Die Dame mit der Maske* (*The Lady with the Mask*). It was to be on the theme of *Inflation*, and this became the title of the piece. In a rapid montage, banknotes pile up in heaps, while the objects they can buy decline in value. Multiplying numbers represent the hundreds, thousands, millions of marks needed in exchange for a single dollar. A fat businessman contrasts with rows of faces of the poor. An investor is reduced to begging. Despite or perhaps due to the fact that it was dealing with a situation that was real in Germany, this sequence was a great success with the public, and other introductions followed: *Rennsymphonie*, a long but interesting impressionistic study of people going to a horse race, and *Two Pence Magic*, a short made to promote a magazine, constructed completely in visual rhymes: a magician introduces the show and invites his audience to see the moon through his telescope; a sudden change of focus and the moon becomes a man's bald head. Having established the principle, Richter avoids the obvious rhyme—a stealthy figure, a gun, 'Hands-Up!' the victim raises his arms, bare arms of a diver, she dives, becomes a plane, swoops down to land, a bird. . . ! In a sequence that pre-dates Hollywood's play on still images in the thirties, a girl (*Vampires*-like) climbs up a rope. A knife starts to cut the rope above her. The picture freezes. Scissors replace the knife and continue to cut—trimming a still photo for the magazine's cover.

With *Vormittagsspuk* (*Ghosts before Breakfast* 1927–8) Richter returned to the personal film. It is his one consciously Dada work, a 'rhythmical story of the rebellion of some objects (hats, neckties, coffee-cups, etc.) against their daily routine. It might represent a personal view of mine that things are also people, because such a theme pops up here and there in some of my films, even in documentaries. (Why not!)' He completed it in time to be shown at an international music festival at Baden-Baden, and music was composed for it by Paul Hindemith, to be performed by live players, conducted from a rolling score, 'the invention of a Mr Blum'. (Tobis, the German sound film pioneers later bought the film and recorded the track on their two-inch sound film, but this version and all trace of Hindemith's music were destroyed by the Nazis.)

In 1930 he made *Alles dreht sich, Alles bewegt sich* (*Everything Revolves, Everything Moves*), a three-reeler made for Tobis, it was his first film in which sound played an integral part; he used the performers, machines and popular music of a funfair as a source of aural and visual material for a 'fantastic documentary'. A boy-meets-girl story which Richter included in the film has been removed from most existing prints, leaving just a series of brilliant images, optically abstracted from the fairground crowd, and Méliès-like trick performances by the artists. A strong man divides in two to reveal a beautiful girl 'inside'. Together again he walks up the wall (the edge of the frame) and across the ceiling to perform a neat somersault. When he juggles with dumb-bells they take over and jump about in the air by themselves.

Richter possessed a highly developed awareness of images which distinguishes his early work from all other films of the period. The mallet hitting the ground in *Film Study*, seen as a dark silhouette against the black V-shape of the man's trousers, is immediately preceded by a play of multiplied geometric V-shapes and squares; the 'crowd of birds' shot later in the same film is followed by a short sequence of circles spinning in exactly the same 'overall random' configuration; taken together these pairs of images create the same kind of kinetic analogy that interests many West Coast American film-makers today (e.g. Pat O'Neill's oil-pump and dancing girl juxtaposition, see page 140). Similarly, the flow of transformations in *Two Pence Magic* are very closely paralleled by Bruce Conner's *A Movie* (1958).

After 1930 Richter's European output consisted of 'straight documentaries, essay films and commercials, mostly in Holland and Switzerland'. Despite the popular success of *Everything Revolves, Everything Moves*, his early films were attacked by the rising Nazi party. This was no doubt partly aggravated by his championing of the Deutsche Liga für unabhängigen Film (German League for the Independent Film), an organization founded in 1929 to 'fight against the glorification of war and the encroachments of censorship', which arranged screenings of avant-garde films followed by discussion. A physical attack upon Richter by two Nazis was reported by the press and led to a commission from a Berlin company, Prometheur-Film, to make an anti-Nazi film *Metal*, about a metal workers' strike in Henningsdorf: 'It was an ill-starred venture, because it tried to follow the political problems of the morning, which had changed already in the evening.' It was finally shelved in 1933 when Hitler came to power. In 1940 Richter emigrated to the United States.

Walter Ruttmann, like Eggeling and Richter, started his career as an artist. Well known in Munich for his engravings and lithographs, he began to make abstract animated films in the early twenties. There the similarity ends. Unlike Eggeling and Richter,

Ruttmann's career brought him success almost immediately. His first works—a series of *Opera* (*Opus 1, 2, 3* etc.; 1922–4) were made using 'a small structure with turning horizontal sticks' on which plasticine forms were mounted. They were illuminated from above to reveal only their top surfaces, which could easily be moved between takes. *Opus 1,* 'a dynamic display of spots vaguely recalling x-ray photographs', was hand-coloured to enhance the effect and created quite a sensation when shown in Berlin in 1922. Between 1923 and 1926 Ruttmann designed 'magic and cloud effects' for Lotte Reiniger's feature length cut-out silhouette animation *The Adventures of Prince Achmed,* then radically changed his style to make another commissioned work, Kriemhild's *Dream of Hawks*—a short animated heraldic design in which two black hawks attack a white dove, for Fritz Lang's *Die Nibelungen* (1924).

In 1927 he was chosen, in recognition of his 'sense of optical music' to edit a film that had been devised some two years earlier by Carl Mayer (scénariste of *Caligari*, *The Last Laugh*, *Sunrise*, etc.) and already largely photographed by Karl Freund (cameraman on *The Last Laugh*, *Vaudeville*, etc.). This was *Berlin, die Symphonie einer Grossstadt* (*Berlin, the Symphony of a Great City*).

Mayer and Freund were both anxious to break with the studio-bound tradition of the German film industry—they had set out to confront reality in a 'melody of pictures'. 'I wanted to show everything,' Mayer recalled in an interview (*Popular Photography* 1939), 'men getting up to go to work, eating breakfast, boarding trams or walking. My characters were drawn from all the walks of life. From the lowest labourer to the bank president.' Freund devised a number of candid camera techniques to assist his work. Using stock which he had hypersensitized (to compensate for poor lighting conditions) he mounted the camera in a 'half-enclosed truck with slots in the sides for the lens' and on one occasion placed it in an innocent looking box and carried it around like a suitcase (devices 'rediscovered', for example, by Billy Wilder for *The Lost Weekend* and by Jean-Luc Godard for *A Bout de Souffle*).

But the film in its complete form became Ruttmann's. His editing technique concentrated exclusively on the surface (a very beautiful surface as the stills reveal, plates 16 to 22); he composed his images according to their visual dynamic to form a succession of pleasing sensations; the function or condition of the objects shown has no particular significance. The poor, the rich and zoo animals are shown eating their lunch and little more is revealed about them than the mechanical similarity of their actions. Comparison with Cavalcanti's film about Paris made a few months earlier, *Rien que les Heures*, emphasizes this. Despite his overly sentimental treatment, Cavalcanti admits the presence of individual emotions within the city by linking his images to specific personal incidents. Emotion is represented in Ruttmann's film by two pairs of anonymous legs, one male, one female, seen heading for a hotel door. Richter, living in Berlin at the time, was not entirely sympathetic:

> Whatever there is to say against *Berlin* this film was a work of art . . . impressionistic art! That is where the critics caught up with Ruttmann. Impressionism was a vision of yesterday, was dead as philosophy. '*Berlin*, vue à travers un temperament' was unsatisfactory and revolting to people who had grown up to understand more about the soul and problems of the big city that Ruttmann showed. The splendid musical rhythm of the pictures seemed abused, and ran suddenly in a vacuum.

But the film was enormously successful with the public; Berliners received it as a great tribute.

Ruttmann described his early animations as 'optical music'; *Berlin* was the first German feature to have a complete orchestral score written specifically to accompany it; the occurance of sound was therefore a significant event in his life. Germany had one of the best sound recording systems, the Vogt, Massol and Engel 'Triergon' process which the Tobis company patented. In 1928 Ruttmann was given access to this equipment and made *Wochenende* (*Weekend*) a film with no pictures, just a sound montage, recording the noises of a working day and a Sunday in the countryside. This time Richter felt more enthusiastic: 'It was a symphony of sound, speech fragments and silence woven into a poem. If I had to choose between all of Ruttmann's works, I would give this one the prize as the most inspired. It re-created with perfect ease in sound the principles of picture poetry which was the characteristic of the absolute film.' For once, Richter seems to be wildly off the track. The essence of the 'absolute film', as demonstrated by Eggeling's *Diagonal Symphony* and Richter's own *Rhythmus* series, is in its reduction of the 'drama' to 'absolute' visual (kinetic) terms—to an abstraction in other words. *Weekend* would seem to be the very opposite of abstract—being an 'impression' of a period of time passing, relying on specific associations—a train starting, a cock crowing—and empathy, to keep the audience in touch with what was happening. (Perhaps the first 'absolute' sound film was made in the 1960s by the American film-maker, Paul Haines, *An All Ethnic Electric Program*—a curious but very beautiful work. It follows three minutes of obliquely seen 'natural' objects—the last image is of a baby rabbit sitting on a slice of bread—with forty minutes of 'abstract' sound, not 'music' but an absolute sound-track, consisting of fragmented and complete vocal noises, instrumental noises, broadcast noise, etc.)

In the same year (1928) Ruttmann made a commercial short, *Tonende Welle* (*Sounding Wave*), which 'surveyed the world of sound offered by radio', then in 1930 he started work on his ultimate collage film *Die Melodie der Welt* (*World Melody*). Perhaps predictably it was a vast piece of 'pop philosophy'—an attempt to show the basic unity of man's behaviour, and the areas in which conflict arises (religious belief was the chief offender in Ruttmann's opinion—he totally ignores social inequality). However, *World Melody* had at least one redeeming feature, it gave work to Oskar Fischinger (on a brief animated sequence) during a lean period.

During the thirties Ruttmann became involved with the Nazi party, making more 'city films' (for Stuttgart and Hamburg), and a political piece *Stahl* (*Steel*) followed by a Pirandello screenplay *Acciaio* for Mussolini in Italy. He also collaborated on films with Abel Gance (*Fin du Monde* 1931) and Leni Riefenstahl (*Olympiade* 1936–7) before concentrating on making political documentaries. He was killed on the German–Russian front in 1941.

The films of Oskar Fischinger continued Ruttmann's early exploration of 'optical music' into the thirties. Though Fischinger's work was to have most impact in post-war America (see page 53), it is interesting to note that both he and Laszlo Moholy-Nagy experimented with the direct manipulation of the sound-track during the early thirties and that their experiments were shown in London at the Film Society where Len Lye and later Norman McLaren were able to see them. (Norman McLaren made his first drawn soundtrack, *Allegro*, in 1939.)

Fischinger's *Experiments in Hand Drawn Sound* (1931), which he described as 'patterns drawn on paper with pen and ink, photographed on to the margin of the film reserved for the sound-track', was first shown in 1932. In 1933 Moholy-Nagy, who had been a master at the Bauhaus, made his *ABC of Sound*, which he described as 'a lighthearted experiment'. In it he indicates the difference in sound produced by the 'arbitrary manipulation' of the soundtrack. 'Every change in the pattern of the track whether typography, profile or other design is immediately audible.' The soundtrack was rephotographed for simultaneous projection on to the screen. Moholy-Nagy showed his *ABC of Sound* to the Film Society in 1934, a year before he moved to London. He remained in London until the founding of the New Bauhaus in Chicago in 1937.

Lenin's nationalization of the Russian film industry soon after 1917 meant that experimental developments could only take place within its structure—independent production during the twenties would have been unthinkable. The ideas originated by Dziga Vertov, Lev Kuleshov and Sergei Eisenstein, working within the industry, contributed to the world-wide restructuring of the narrative film and had considerable effect on a number of 'personal' film-makers both before and after the war.

In an interview with Stephen P. Hill (*Film Culture* 44), Kuleshov confirms the view of most historians, that it was through seeing early American films (the work of Griffith, Chaplin, etc.) that the Russians recognized the power of editing. He defines his contribution:

> I was asked the question: am I or is Griffith the inventor of editing? I answered that of course the first editing (montage) of pictures, the first close-ups, I saw in Griffith's pictures. But Griffith did it to some extent subconsciously—he did it simply as an artist (it was natural for him to do that). So I was the first director to give conscious thought to why editing is essential in the cinema.

As early as 1919 Kuleshov started to make radical experiments in the use of editing. While working on official newsreels he conducted the famous test that came to be known as the 'Kuleshov effect':

> From old films I took shots of the actor Mozhukhin and edited them with various other shots. At first, I had Mozhukhin seeming to sit still in jail and then he was gladdened by the sun, the landscape and the freedom which he found. In another combination I had Mozhukhin sitting in the same position, in the same attitude, and looking at a half-naked woman. In another combination he looked at a child's coffin—there were many different combinations. And in all those cases, so far as the expression on Mozhukhin's face was concerned, it had the very same significance which I gave it in my editing.

A year later, while assisting at the First National Film school, he experimented with 'creative geography' (Jay Leyda's phrase) in which he constructed a satisfactory 'single location' for his actors, out of shots taken at different places all over Moscow. He also created a single 'ideal' woman from the features of a group of girls. This conscious exploitation of the camera's ability to lie led to more than a reappraisal of cinematic credibility—it meant a new involvement in the schematic presentation of the art of editing. 'Montage' as developed by Kuleshov and his pupils, Pudovkin and Eisenstein, was not just 'a series of connecting shocks arranged in a certain sequence and directed at the audience' (Eisenstein's aggressive definition), it was very much the formal art form of a group of aesthetes. Robert Nelson's 'informal' montage in the 1960s (see page 146) emphasizes this without detracting from the truth of Kuleshov's observations.[1]

Like Kuleshov, Dziga Vertov was schooled on newsreel photography and editing, but managed to make a virtue out of necessity. As early as 1916 Vertov had been interested in montage—sound montage—and had set up a rudimentary sound studio in Petrograd where he could make 'music' by the arrangement and re-recording of collected sounds. Then in 1918, through his work as editor of the weekly newsreel *Kino Nedelia* (movieweek), he began to formulate his ideas about the representation of reality on the screen. While endorsing Kuleshov's montage theories (to the extent of paraphrasing them as his own in his manifestoes), Vertov was completely opposed to the 'American' concept of movie-making with its director, plot, artificial sets, actors, etc., which Kuleshov upheld in Russia. In his *Manifesto* (1920) and *Resolution of the Council of Three* (1923) he stresses his belief in the camera's superiority to the human eye in its ability to select (by directing the attention and editing), to condense time (by cutting and fast motion) and to combine diverse elements into a single visual experience (superimposition and montage). He demands that the camera's potential in these fields be exploited to illuminate 'life as it is':

> *Way of the machine*
> The initial point: the utilization of the camera as a cinema eye —more perfect than a human eye for the purposes of research into the chaos of visual phenomena filling the universe.

[1] Karl Freund gives this curious account of the origins of Russian-montage: 'Eisenstein and Pudovkin have both told me that when the Soviet Film Trust was first formed there was not only little or no equipment with which to work, but there was actually no money with which to buy film! When at last some money was available, there was still very little of it; so the Soviet cameramen and directors would send down to Berlin to buy "short ends" from the German studios—little bits of five, ten and fifteen feet of film—left in the camera magazines after we had made our scenes. Rarely did they have the luck to obtain more than twenty feet of film in a single piece; naturally they had to adapt their techniques to utilize these extremely short bits of film—and utilize them efficiently.' Karl Freund, 'What is montage' *American Cinematographer* 1934.

Accidental synthesis and concentration of motion
To this day the cameraman is criticized if a running horse moves unnaturally slowly on the screen (quick turn of the camera) or, conversely, if a tractor ploughs too fast (the slow manipulation of the camera crank). These of course are incidental, but we are preparing a thought-out system of these incidents, a system of apparent abnormalities which organize and explore phenomena.

Do not copy from the eyes
To this day we raped the movie camera and forced it to copy the work of our eye. And the better the copy, the better the shot was considered. As of today we will unshackle the camera and will make it work in the opposite direction, further from copying.

Vertov's group called themselves Kinoks; their film-magazine *Kino-Pravda,* an extension of their principles into a newsreel format, ran to twenty issues (1923–5). But their most complete statements are contained in *Kino Glaz, Jizn Vrasplokh* (*Film Eye, Life with the Unexpected* 1924), whose title implies 'shooting without knowledge of the people filmed', and the celebrated *Man with a Movie Camera* (1929). Being entirely 'original' footage and containing no political message as such, *Man with a Movie Camera* is naturally the most accessible of these works in non-communist countries and as a result has become something of an avant-garde classic. However, in comparison to the earlier works or to *Enthusiasm* (*Donbass Symphony* 1930) and *Three Songs of Lenin* (1934), its subject and camera trickery appear somewhat self-conscious in their virtuosity.

Vertov is regarded as the father of the English documentary and of the *cinéma vérité* movement. Godard and his political followers have claimed his influence. Vertov's awareness of the potential enhancement of images by 'unnatural' and chance occurrences is equally vital to the working procedure of many so-called underground film-makers such as Ron Rice, Stan Brakhage and Ken Jacobs. The reworking of images in *Three Songs of Lenin,* for example, the repetition and re-contexting of a shot containing an awkward but revealing gesture of Lenin's, is closely paralleled by Brakhage's treatment of his 'mountain man' figure in *Dog Star Man.*

In 1929 members of the European avant-garde movement gathered on an international scale. A congress was organized at the Chateau de la Sarraz in Switzerland by Robert Aron and

Jeannine Bouissounouse, calling together representatives of independent cinema from thirteen countries. England sent Cavalcanti and Isaacs from the Film Society; France, Bela Balasz (the Marxist film theoretician), Leon Moussinac and representatives of the Film Club movement; Hans Richter and Walter Ruttmann represented Germany; Eisenstein, Tisse and Alexandroff represented Russia; and delegates from the Film Liga of Holland, the cine clubs of Switzerland and Spain, and similar organizations in Italy, Japan, etc. were present.

The purpose was to establish an international league of cine clubs that would 'help those who struggled to promote the independent film', and an 'international co-operative' in Paris, to 'promote films without commercial concessions of any sort, creations that were resolutely dedicated to human values and the poetry of the cinema'.

The debate was lively. The Soviets explained that in a capitalist system the concept of 'independent cinema' was a fiction of the same order as the 'free press'. The Italian 'Futurist' delegate loudly defended the involvement of his group in Mussolini's movement, but much of the time was spent in the constructive discussion of the proposed league's administrative procedure.

The delegates showed their latest films; Richter, Eisenstein and Montagu made a brief film *The Storming of La Sarraz* in which the delegates, disguised as 'Commerce' and 'Independence', battled for the 'spirit of the artistic film'.

The congress disbanded in goodwill, with a resolution to meet again in Brussels the following year. By 1930, however, the political scene in Europe had entirely changed and most avant-garde film-makers had ceased production. Those that attended the Brussels congress dissolved the 'Internationale' after the members of 'all fourteen participating countries [except Italy and Spain] explained their desire to use the film more as a weapon in the fight against fascism'.

TRANSITIONAL ANIMATORS

After 1930 the European avant-garde virtually ceased to exist; it was only in one field—animation—that experimental film-makers continued to be active. These remaining film-artists were few in number and they usually worked in isolation. With the exception of Berthold Bartosch, whose connexions with the avant-garde encouraged him to continue his dependence on private patronage and art-house audiences, most of these animators cultivated relationships with business organizations and the film-industry itself—partly because of the shortage of private finance and, more positively, because the sponsored film and cinema commercial offered a chance to work with sophisticated sound and colour equipment long before it became generally available. For over twenty years, in fact until the advent of television, the cinema commercial was to provide the working context for most aspiring experimental film-makers in Europe; few survived it.

Bartosch completed only one major film in the forty years of his active life. In his devotion to his work and his concern to avoid commercial exploitation of his techniques, he anticipates such 'loners' as Harry Smith and Douglas Crockwell in post-war America. It was as a student of architecture in Vienna that Bartosch first became involved in film. His tutor, Professor Hazlink, encouraged his interest in movies; Hazlink believed in the educational role of the movies and stressed that film experiences become an active part of the viewer's subconscious. Under his guidance Bartosch made several films to illustrate Masaryk's philosophy—*Le Communism*, *L'Humanité* and others (*c.* 1914–20).

Bartosch later moved to Berlin, where he worked with Ruttmann on Lotte Reiniger's *The Adventures of Prince Achmed* (1923–6); he also met Jean Renoir (with whom he collaborated briefly) and Kafka's publisher Kurt Wolff. It was Wolff who suggested that he attempt an animated version of Masereel's book of propagandist woodcuts *Une Idée*. Initially Bartosch and Masereel were to collaborate, Masereel designing and Bartosch animating, but there were disagreements and the plan fell through.

In 1929 Bartosch moved to Paris; Tedesco gave him a tiny space in Le Vieux Colombier in which to build his animation bench, which was in effect the first 'multiplane camera', though it was not given that name until the Disney Studios reinvented it in 1938. With it he began to work on his own version of the abandoned film, drawing and re-drawing on each layer of glass a frame at a time. For the hard-edged shapes in the foreground he used cardboard cut-outs, but most of the designs he drew directly on to the glass, using a black grease crayon and white soap as pigments. Each layer was lit from below by only 30 watts of light—just enough to make the soap glow, but requiring that each frame be given a lengthy exposure. The resulting images have an extraordinary luminosity and depth. The camera shutter was opened and timed by a trigger mechanism constructed out of a bicycle pump and a series of weights. (Alexandre Alexeieff, when building his own rostrum a few years later, made an exact copy of this part of the design, but was very disappointed with the inaccuracy of his first exposures. Revisiting Bartosch he discovered that the original pump had been precisely calibrated to fiftieths of a second.)

The subject of *L'Idée* (the title under which the film was released in 1931) is one of revolutionary struggle. 'The idea', represented by the figure of a naked woman, is created by an artist and sent forth to disseminate its message. Rejected by businessman and bureaucrat, she is adopted by a young militant and together they try to rouse the oppressed workers to rebellion. They are met with further opposition and the militant is shot. The film ends with scenes of war, with 'l'idée' hovering over the dead and dying. In theme it is similar to Gance's *J'Accuse.*

The English director Thorold Dickinson undertook to produce a second film projected by Bartosch based on his ideas about the cosmos. Though he reported that various scenes had been completed, the new film was still not finished at the time of his death in 1969, and he left no trace of it.

Alexandre Alexeieff and his wife Clair Parker were close friends of Bartosch. However, they supported themselves almost entirely by making commercials. Cinema commercials were the life blood of the French short film-makers (more so than anywhere else in Europe), and the standard of their productions was comparably higher. Alexeieff himself, like Ruttmann, was an engraver/lithographer and only became interested in film-making after seeing Fernand Léger's *Ballet Mécanique.* His first and most powerful work was an 'illustration' of Mussorgsky's *Une Nuit sur le Mont Chauve* (*Night on the Bare Mountain* 1934). To make it, he and Clair Parker invented the 'pin screen'—a board covered with 500,000 pins which could be raised or lowered by hand or by using a small roller—the effect is close to mezzotinting, the light and shade in this instance being created by the height of the pins. The screen was changed and photographed one frame at a time.

In 1935 Alexeieff made the first Gasparcolor film in France—*La Belle au Bois Dormant.* Unable to use the pin screen for colour work, he resorted to using puppet animation. Most of his commissioned works during the thirties were made in this way. Only in 1943 when John Grierson invited him and Clair Parker to go to Canada were they able to continue their earlier experiments.

On a second screen (with 1,000,000 pins) they made *En Passant* (1943; plate 23), a fable about the animals of the field, for NFBC's Chants Populaires series. The extraordinary image mutations which the pin screen allows were probably most widely seen in the 'Man at the Gate' prologue to Orson Welles' version of *The Trial* (1962).

There is nothing technically to prevent the pins from changing their apparent brightness as fast as the dots on a television screen, but Alexeieff's technique suggests almost slow-motion—the difference between images being almost as important and involving as the images themselves. In 1951 Alexeieff started work on a new series of films using 'pendules composés', a technique he described as follows:

> We construct robots controlled by compound pendulums or motor-powered mechanisms, which themselves control the movement in space of a 'tracer', a small luminous object (a drop of glass—lit by a strobe). These tracer movements are recorded on a single frame by a long exposure, and form a 'totalized' solid. Then, after changing the parameters which govern the robot, a fresh series of trace movements is recorded on another frame—and so on. The degree of condensation is such that a final film of one minute may represent twelve hours of the tracer's movement. What is animated is not a natural solid, but a 'totalized' or illusory solid. Although this technique is used to sell coffee, petrol or cigarettes, it also aims at widening our metaphysical concept of the world.

Sève de la Terre (1955) is typical of this advertising work. In the centre of a desert the letters 'ESSO' rotate and disappear into the ground. In their place an 'oil tree' grows—a derrick in the shape of a flowering bush. From its branches luminous drops appear, fall and burn with a white flame as they hit the ground. A single drop—trembles—changes colour—vibrates into luminiscent patterns. The patterns form the letters 'ESSO' again, drops appear beneath each letter—they too fall. A pealing of church bells is heard throughout.

Recently Alexeieff returned to the pin screen to make *Le Nez* (1963) from the story by Gogol.

During the early forties the Whitney brothers had begun their work using pendulums to create synthetic soundtracks (see page 56). Alexeieff was enthusiastic but slightly envious of their freedom: 'It is good to know that an artist like John Whitney in California is able to work with "pendules composés" even though no market has opened itself to him.' Whitney recently described his own feeling about the graphic uses of the pendulum; it was the pendulum's inability to exactly repeat a movement, despite careful control of the parameters, and the laboriousness of the techniques involved, that led him to use the analogue computer, which was being developed at that time for use in automatic gun positioning (see page 57).

Len Lye is one of the few significant figures in British cinema between the wars. He is as important to personal (informal) animation as Griffith is to the traditional narrative film. Lye's achievement was to free animation from the 'mechanical' frame by frame process—making it as direct and immediate in its creation of images as 'live' photography.

As a child in New Zealand, he built simple three-dimensional models to study kinetics, then left for Australia where he studied animation. Coming to England in 1927, he persuaded the Film Society to pay for the photography of his first film *Tusalava* (which he completed, with further financial assistance from Robert Graves, in 1929). A straightforward animation of 'aboriginal' shapes, he has described it as 'the slowest thing on earth'—and it was six years before he next attempted a film. This time he worked directly on the surface of rejected sound takes (clear film with only the soundtrack printed), given to him by professional film-makers (members of the Film Society). Having completed a certain amount of this material, he showed it to John Grierson of the GPO film unit, suggesting that with the insertion of suitable slogans, it could be used as a GPO promotional film. Much to his surprise, Grierson agreed. So *Colour Box* (1935; plate 25)—the first non-camera film—was seen by a larger public than any experimental film before it, and most since.

In 1947 Cavalcanti wrote (*Sight and Sound*, vol. 16, 1964): '*Colour Box* is a very important film, not only because of its successful use of colour, but also because it is a demonstration of the rhythm created on the screen by the succession of lines composing each individual frame or group of frames. Eisenstein in his book *Film Sense* takes much more time and much more pains to explain the same thing that *Colour Box* throws at you so naturally, and does so in less than three minutes.'

Thereafter most of Lye's English films were made for Grierson and the Post Office. With *Birth of a Robot* (1935/6) he turned to puppet animation in a film resembling the work of George Pal (a popular English puppet animator who made advertising films in England, became resident artist to Philips in Holland and eventually ended up in Hollywood). It contains an 'abstract' storm sequence but proved to be a dead end otherwise.

In *Rainbow Dance* (1936; plate 24) Lye introduced the human figure:

> I always wanted to do a live action film. My area of imagery is only concerned with the sensory side of bodily being and what they call neuromotor, nerve muscle stuff, which is the area of dance, but I'm not that interested in dance . . . I wasn't interested at all in naturalistic work. What I was interested in

was the way of taking . . . real live action in the studio, under circumstances in which your understanding of motion would be such that you could break that motion right down and build it up again in cinema terms, kinetic terms.

Rainbow Dance also exploits the flexibility of the (Technicolor) principle of combining three differing black and white records (colour separations) to form the full colour print. The varying density of each black and white record determines the hue of the final print. Thus 'all the significant colours, whether attached to objects taken from reality or to abstracted shapes, are conceived and composed directly in terms of the Gasparcolor dye'. Lye described the film: 'A city man is seen standing in the rain; the rain stops and he goes off on his holiday. The Post Office Savings Bank puts a pot of gold at the end of the rainbow.' Lye combines recognizable rainbows with a negative shot of a girl's head, formalized shots of sea and sky and the 'city man' (Robert Doone) 'executing symbolic ballet movements'. Compared with Maya Deren's use of camera and dance movements, especially in *Choreography for Camera*, Lye's 'image consciousness' becomes very apparent. Deren's emphasis on the continuity between camera and dance movements does not concern Lye—he enjoys the kinetic evolution of the film (a concern much closer to the current West Coast school of film-making). In *Swinging the Lambeth Walk* (1939), he stresses this 'link with the future' by his use of the optical printer and colour mattes. With the advent of war, Lye was commissioned to make 'straight' documentaries; in 1944 he left for New York to work for the *March of Time* producers. He continued his own work with *Colour Cry* (1952), *Rhythm* (1953) and *Free Radicals* (1958). In this last work Lye returned to the direct manipulation of the film stock, greatly simplifying the earlier process by eliminating the various stages of application and printing, in favour of a direct scratching of the film emulsion with the equivalent of engraving tools. The 'signatures' produced in this way, he edited down to a sequence of deceptively simple evolutions—their subtlety only becoming apparent after repeated viewings.

After *Free Radicals* Lye publically announced his withdrawal from film as a medium, and his intention to concentrate on kinetic sculpture (some of which he contributed to the Fourth Experimental Film Festival at Knokke-Le-Zoute, Belgium, in 1968). However, he did work on another 'scratch' film, *Particles in Space*, between 1961 and 1966.

America between the wars

The European avant-garde, particularly in France, was relatively independent of the commercial structure of the film industry, but in America there was no such clear-cut separation until after the second world war—independent film-makers during the twenties and thirties fought for the commercial distribution of their films, and if they failed (as most did) they accepted the fact, feeling there was little they could do about it.

But the avant-garde movement as such accounts for only a small proportion of the experimental work carried out in the USA during this period. During the late twenties and early thirties Hollywood and the film equipment industry developed an enormous number of technical innovations that were to extend the whole potential of cinematography. Many of these techniques, developed to further the aims of the narrative film, have only now come within the economic range of the experimental film-maker. The optical printer, for example, was designed during the thirties and used extensively to create both sophisticated transitions from one sequence to another, and 'super-realities' combined from separate (often improbable) visual ingredients. Only in the last five years have 'amateurs', like Scott Bartlett and Pat O'Neill, been able to suggest its creative potential. Hollywood's craftsmen and technicians—the men responsible for the invention and development of studio machinery—have largely gone unacknowledged. The custom of crediting the director with complete 'auteurship' persists. This may be justifiable in the case of such total directors as Eric von Stroheim and Josef von Sternberg, but the style and visual integrity of many otherwise unexceptional Hollywood pictures is often due to the editor or the cameraman. The success of the final sequence of *The Charge of the Light Brigade* is due rather to B. Reeves Eason's 'direction of horse action' and George Amy's editing than to Michael Curtiz' direction.

More immediately recognizable are the entire sequences created by Hollywood 'specialists', for example: Busby Berkeley's dance sequences; montages created by Vorkapich; Byron Haskin's special effects. These technicians and effects men were forced to specialize in one field, risking redundancy should their particular styling go out of fashion. Tragically, their own medium—the Hollywood narrative film—made sustained achievement impossible; their *œuvre* exists as a series of 'high-spots'—visually intelligent sequences and optical day-dreams—in otherwise nondescript melodramas. At their best these 'specialists' succeeded in creating an original cinematic language and a concept of visual phantasmagoria that set standards for the cinema-educated film-makers of the post-war years.

AVANT-GARDE FILM-MAKERS 1921–34

An active critical movement of critics, directors and audiences was able to sustain Europe's most inventive film-artists, but America offered no such support. As a result most American avant-garde production was the work of professionals working within the film industry who attempted 'on the side' to emulate European achievements. America's most active avant-garde period (1928–32) followed immediately on that of Europe (1924–8).

America's first avant-garde film was Charles Sheeler's and Paul Strand's *Manhatta*, an isolated attempt made as early as 1921. A film-visualization of a poem about New York by Walt Whitman, it punctuates the rather static, but beautifully photographed shots of city structures with titles taken from Whitman's verses. It is a film without human characters; Sheeler—a prominent 'modern' painter—and Strand—a progressive photographer—concentrated on the existing visual beauty of selected images and showed no evidence of any interest in movie-visual (kinetic) expression (as proposed in Delluc's contemporary theory of *Photogénie*, for example).

In 1925, Robert Flaherty made a film with a similar theme—*24 Dollar Island*—again excluding the human element, but revealing Flaherty's instinctive sense of filmic pictorial composition. *24 Dollar Island*, he maintained, was virtually an essay in the use of the long-focus lens, which allowed him to make close-ups of architectural detail from a great distance. The success of this experiment encouraged him to use similar lenses in his subsequent feature films—an excellent example being the shots of the small boat in a storm at sea in *Man of Aran* (1934). This short film, however, never achieved the popularity of his previous *Nanook of the North* (1919) and ended up being projected in a cut-down version as the backdrop to a live stage show at New York's Roxy Cinema.

German Expressionist films were soon to make a strong impact in America, leading to a burst of *Caligari*-like film-making. Such activity largely took place in Hollywood where several German directors (Lubitsch, Murnau, Lupu Pick, Paul Leni) were already working. The first to make this kind of film were Slavko Vorkapich and Robert Florey, with their tragicomic tale of the frustrations of an extra trying to break into the 'star system'—*The Life and Death of 9413—A Hollywood Extra*. Vorkapich, an immigrant from Belgrade, had been working in Hollywood since 1922 when he wrote the screenplay for Rex Ingram's *The Prisoner of Zenda*. He continued to experiment within the context of the Hollywood film until his return to Yugoslavia in the early fifties. (Ultimately he returned to California to accept an academic post.)

Florey had an even more varied career. Born in Paris, as a child he was a frequent visitor to Monsieur and Madame Méliès and later became assistant to Louis Feuillade, acting opposite René Clair in Feuillade's twenty-four episode *L'Orpheline* (1921). Through Clair he met Louis Delluc and his circle and was introduced to the American and German film. He emigrated to Hollywood in 1921 and established himself first as a gag writer and then as 'director of foreign publicity' for the Pickford–Fairbanks household. He then worked as assistant to a number of well-known directors, including von Sternberg and King Vidor. Offers of directorships then started to come from several independent 'quickie-film' producers, but Florey had an interesting reason for refusing them: he recalls, 'I couldn't *afford* to be a director for the independent studios. Columbia and Tiffany paid $175–200 a picture and that included editing it. A good assistant at the majors got $250 a week and was assured of months of employment.' Similar motives have led others to follow Florey's example of working for the major studios in order to make their own films, but few ever realize their ambition.

A Hollywood Extra was made largely in Vorkapich's house and cost only $96. The two central characters, the Extra and Mr Blank, a successful star, are side-lit and isolated against dark backgrounds to emphasize their conceptual roles. The exteriors and interiors are represented by cut-out silhouettes and miniature open-frame scaffolding constructions—their visual interest being increased by the use of a single moving light-source and occasional rapid subjective camera movements (though no montage as such was included). Greg Toland (cameraman on Orson Welles' *Citizen Kane*) shot the close-ups and the film was originally synchronized to Gershwin's *Rhapsody in Blue*. Ironically, Florey's own connexions in Hollywood helped him find distribution outlets for the picture. Charlie Chaplin arranged a screening for a number of influential friends and secured it an opening on Broadway and a circuit release afterwards.

Florey made three further experimental films between 1927 and 1928—*The Loves of Zero*, *Johann the Coffin Maker* (both indebted to *Caligari*) and *Skyscraper Symphony* (in the 'city symphony' genre). None of them had anything like the success of *A Hollywood Extra*. *Zero* was distinguished only by its sets—the design of William Cameron Menzies (art director of *The Thief of Baghdad* and director of *Things to Come*).

However, on the strength of the success of *A Hollywood Extra*, Florey was offered several short experimental sound assignments by Paramount. Subsequently he directed the Marx Brothers' first film, *The Cocoanuts* (1929), wrote the screenplay of the original *Frankenstein* (1931) and directed numerous 'well made' 'B' pictures before devoting himself to television features. His involvement with the avant-garde was not particularly long-lasting.

Another German-influenced experimental film made in Hollywood during this period was the six-reel *The Last Moment* (1928), made by Paul Fejos (from Hungary, where the film industry had already collapsed) and Leon Shamroy. Lewis Jacobs describes it as a 'study in subjectivity'. The story is:

> based on the theory that at the critical moment before a person loses consciousness he may see a panorama of pictures summarizing the memories of a lifetime. The film opens with a shot of troubled water. A struggling figure is seen. A hand reaches up 'as if in entreaty'. A man is drowning. This scene is followed by a sequence of rapid shots: the head of a Pierrot, faces of women, flashing headlights, spinning wheels, a star shower, an explosion, climaxed by a shot of a child's picture book.
>
> From the book the camera flashes back to summarize the drowning man's life: impressions of school days, a fond mother, an unsympathetic father, a birthday party, reading Shakespeare, a first visit to the theatre . . .

Piece by piece the man's reasons for suicide become apparent. *The Last Moment* was widely distributed and proved to be a box-office success. While establishing its makers' ability to direct it gave little indication of their future intentions. Fejos graduated to directing minor pictures for Universal (incidentally perfecting the camera-crane for his picture *Broadway* in 1929). He later returned to Europe and directed documentaries. Shamroy became 'personal cameraman' to actress Sylvia Sydney for a time, and later the first cameraman to shoot a conventional wide-screen (Cinemascope) picture—*The Robe* (1953).

Although resembling *The Last Moment* in plot construction, *The Spy* (1931–2) by UFA-trained Charles Vidor, made more of a stylistic breakthrough. Vidor adapted the Ambrose Bierce story of a condemned man's fantasy of escape at the moment of death (closely resembling Robert Enrico's remake of 1962—*La Rivière du Hibou* or *Incident at Owl Creek*) and shot it entirely on location, using non-professional actors and straightforward camera movements to stress the 'naturalness' and 'reality' of the fantasy—thus adding to the impact of the ending (the return to the moment of death). However, *The Spy* was to be the only film that Vidor made outside the conventional feature film format. His later works included the Rita Hayworth vehicles—*Cover Girl* (1944) and *Gilda* (1946).

Because of their continued dedication to the experimental film, college professors Dr James Sibley Watson and Melville Webber, working in Rochester, New York, were the first truly avant-garde American film-makers. Their film *The Fall of the House of Usher* (1928) is consistently more inventive and imaginative than Epstein's French version of the same year. They reduced the story to its essentials, the impact being largely transmitted through the careful use of silhouette, multiple exposure and rhythm, which successfully evoke the disembodied atmosphere of the piece. Lady Usher's 'resurrection', for example, is shown as a montage of feet climbing two superimposed flights of white stairs. Sets are suggested by light and by the patterns made by folded paper rather than by painted or three-dimensional props.

Collaborating again, Watson and Webber were to make one of the first American sound experimental films *Lot in Sodom* (1933; plate 26). Significantly, they avoided a direct representation of the sexual conflict implicit in the Biblical story and showed instead a series of symbolic quasi-erotic tableaux that emphasize the elemental qualities of the story. Compared with the more overt treatment of similar themes by Kenneth Anger, Curtis Harrington and Gregory Markopoulos in the forties, its handling of sexuality now seems painfully obscure; at the time, however, its subject matter was considered too much in advance of popular taste to permit commercial distribution. Shot on 35 mm, it was not available to amateur (16 mm) markets either.

However, *Movie Makers*, the magazine of the Amateur Cinema League, nominated *Lot in Sodom* as one of their ten best films of 1933 saying:

> *Lot* represents a complete innovation, not only in the treatment of the theme as a whole, but in the cinematic interpretation of the sequences. The familiar tools of the avant-garde cinema: multiple exposure, trick printing, complicated lighting, symbolism, models and models in combination with life-size sets are used to secure an entirely new and cinematic representation of the Biblical story. In *Lot* these two amateurs have mastered the world of illusion of the motion picture, but in doing so, they

have produced more than mere novelty; they have founded a new cinematic art.

Also working on the East Coast, New York photographer Ralph Steiner made a series of movie-photographic essays that immediately became popular with, and emulated by, amateur cinematographers. Inspired perhaps by Joris Ivens' classic documentaries (made in Holland the previous year), Steiner's *H_2O* (1929) and *Surf and Seaweed* (1930) concentrated on the rhythmic flow of images abstracted from the movement of water. Like Flaherty, Steiner exploited the potential of the long-focus lens and particularly enjoyed the flatness of the image it created. His *Mechanical Principles* (1931) attempted the same kind of abstraction in machine terms, but the machines he chose were less kinetically impressive.

In 1933, Steiner acted as cameraman on a short experimental film, *Pie in the Sky*, put together by a group of actors, headed by Elia Kazan. Kazan, who had been working with the Group Theatre for some years, led his actors into an extended improvisation using as their location, source of inspiration and props, a local rubbish dump. They made, in effect, the first 'found object' drama. The level of inspiration seems 'stagey' now, when compared with contemporary underground standards (improvisations by Taylor Mead for example, in the works of Ron Rice and others). The theme, the ideal after-life as seen in terms of the archaeology of urban society, develops too smoothly to be completely spontaneous, the shots too well-rehearsed—yet the actors' intuitive response to their environment is real and does communicate. Whatever the film's failings, Kazan acknowledged the potential of the non-scripted confrontation of human beings and their environment as a valid subject for film-makers. (Kazan did not work in the cinema again until 1944—the cameraman on his first feature film *A Tree Grows in Brooklyn* was Leon Shamroy.)

A non-Hollywood film-maker on the West Coast, Herman Weinberg, sometime contributor to *Movie Makers*, made *Autumn Fire* (1930), a film very much in the style of Dimitri Kirsanov. His subject was the anxiety and frustration of two lovers, the atmosphere of the piece being evoked largely through the movement of water, trees, a steamer and a train—metaphors for the coming together of two human figures. Weinberg's treatment is academic perhaps, but he re-emphasized the ability of image movement and montage to convey human emotion.

As the amateur market expanded, perhaps predictably a form of domestic 'city symphony' evolved—consciously artistic records of the film-makers' home towns—inspired by Ruttmann, Vertov, and economy in equal measure. Weinberg's *City Symphony* (1929) was one of the first; Irving Browning's *City of Contrasts* and Jay Leyda's *A Bronx Morning*, Lyn Rigg's *A Day in Santa Fé* and later Frank Stauffacher's *Sausalito* were other notable examples. Although they added little technically or aesthetically to the European originals, they served to popularize the idea that the raw materials of art are available everywhere (even in your own home town), bringing the creative process that much closer to the grass roots.

POPULARIZATION OF FILM-MAKING

The European avant-garde had only begun to consider the collective promotion and distribution of their films in 1929 (through the abortive International League of Cine Clubs). It is surprising, therefore, that in the United States such a league already existed in 1926—before there were any American avant-garde film-makers to support. However, the Amateur Cinema League, as it was called (and its monthly magazine *Movie Makers*), was dedicated to the *amateur* film-maker in the popular sense of the word and in no way set out to represent the avant-garde. One of the league's first officers described the films that concerned them:

> . . . films made for family records, travel movies, experiments in scenic pictures made with artistic intent; tentative and sometimes fully-fledged photoplays, studies of athletic form and records of games—all these of extremely personal character in the non-theatrical film category.

Supporting the league's work in the amateur field, the *American Cinematographer* recorded each successive innovation in studio and laboratory techniques, and featured extensive articles by Hollywood's top technicians on how their work, whether processing, special effects or cartoon animation, could be emulated by the amateur in his own home.

In 1920 the Eastman Kodak Company developed a new standard film gauge—16 mm—of a professional capacity but specially designed for amateur use. Marketed initially in 1923 as black and white stock, sound stocks were added in 1933 and colour in 1934. In Europe 9·5 mm was adopted for the amateur market and for a time its development was slightly more advanced than 16 mm—in terms of the speed of camera lenses and the availability of film stocks. But 9·5 mm equipment existed on a much smaller scale than 16 mm and the Americans' choice of the bigger gauge for the circulation of their feature films in Europe during the second world war swung the balance.

Many of the 16-mm cameras used by independent film-makers today were designed and built in the early thirties—for example, the Bolex used by Gregory Markopoulos to create his extraordinarily complex in-camera editing and superimposition. There was nothing to prevent pre-war amateurs from making similar use of their equipment; perhaps one reason why they did not was the comparative expense of cameras in pre-war years. The amateurs who could afford them, therefore, generally belonged to the successful business class who had little time for anything but the recreational use of their equipment. Cocteau once said, 'The cinema will only become an art when its raw materials are as cheap as pencil and paper.'

As well as the expense of equipment, dissatisfaction with the Hollywood product was as yet unknown, as illustrated by an *American Cinematographer* club-section editorial: 'One reason why movies made by the Long Beach Cinema Club consistently win prizes is because they are produced like movies in Hollywood.'

During the thirties, however, in response to popular interest in European developments, the Amateur Cinema League and a similar organization—the American Film Arts Guild—became involved for a short time in the import and export of avant-garde film programmes, making use of an amendment of the American Tariff laws arranged by the league in 1930, that allowed 'free entry of personal films into the United States under certain conditions'. This recognition of non-commercial film-making did not continue after the war, however. When Stauffacher inaugurated the Art in Cinema series and Deren and Vogel their screenings at the Provincetown Playhouse, neither *Movie Makers* nor the *American Cinematographer* felt obliged to cover the events. During the forties, *Movie Makers* only reviewed films of the *Ramblings in the West*, *Flowers of Erotic Beauty*, *Yosemite Winter* and *The Park* variety. No mention was ever made of more serious film-makers. Although the amateur movement failed to recognize the importance of the new film-makers, it at least provided the American nation with equipment for a non-industrial cinematic revolution.

HOLLYWOOD—INNOVATION AND EXPERIMENT

In an industry devoted to making narrative films which depend upon the direct association and empathy of the public for their success, it was perhaps predictable that conventions similar to those governing the behaviour of the screen characters should also determine the editing process. An obvious example of such a convention was the immediate adoption of D. W. Griffith's cross-cutting device in all subsequent 'race against time' sequences. Even today, students are shown how dialogue should be filmed by alternating close-ups, left to right and back again, with occasional mid- or long-shots to locate the characters.

The full implications of editing—its ability to manipulate the time/space continuum (as demonstrated by Gance, Kuleshov, etc.)—represented a threat to the orderly sequential continuity of the feature film; Hollywood's maxim was that editing should be as inconspicuous as possible. The one exception to this rule in the pre-war period was montage, not Russian montage, but the romantic montage as practised by Vorkapich (see page 47) and others. Even in the post-war period, and until quite recently in fact, audiences have complained of disorientation on the few occasions when directors have broken this rule (for instance, the initial reception of Resnais' *L'Année Dernière à Marienbad*). In contrast avant-garde film-makers since Fernand Léger have always accepted at least the possibility that each frame could be completely different from its predecessor, and may have taken advantage of this freedom. More recently, Markopoulos has demonstrated that no valid reason ever existed for the exclusion of truly creative editing even in the context of the narrative film.

The use and treatment of camera movement *during* a shot has, by comparison, been less stylized, and is one area where the commercial cinema has developed formal techniques to a degree unparalleled, until very recently, by avant-garde film-makers (the reasons being largely economic).

The American director Alan Dwan is currently credited with the invention of the tracking shot, but it was in Germany, in F. W. Murnau's *The Last Laugh* (1924), that extended moving camera techniques were first seriously considered. The whole story of this film was conceived (by script-writer Carl Mayer and photographer Karl Freund) in terms of the camera's progress from one point to another. Instead of just approaching a subject to focus attention on it, they attempted to indicate the emotional state of the central character (the demoted hotel doorman) through the camera's relationship with its surroundings. From its fluid position, whether suspended from tracks on the ceiling or floating in the equivalent of a rolling dolly, the camera was able to make clinically objective observations or to take the doorman's subjective viewpoint according to what each scene required. For Murnau's *Faust* (1926), Freund evoked the aerial flight that Faust takes with Mephistopheles by constructing a roller-coaster over a vast studio-built landscape (complete with villages, etc.), and racing his camera over it.

In Hollywood, Charles Rosher took over as Murnau's cameraman on his best American work, *Sunrise* (1927). Rosher had been to Germany and for *Sunrise* he consciously adopted the use of the overhead tracks he had seen there, building one of the longest tracks ever, over a mile long, for the extraordinary scene of the country lovers' tram ride to the city. In another scene, the camera glides 'impossibly' smoothly over the ground accompanying Janet Gaynor as she stumbles through the woods. The effect is stunning. An action is presented, conceptually, as never before.

The imprisonment of studio cameras with the coming of sound was only temporary, but similar virtuoso performances with sound cameras remained rare. An exception was the musical film —where the complete artificiality of the staged dance routines freed the camera from the microphone boom, allowing more sophisticated movement (each sequence had to be post-synced anyway). The work of Busby Berkeley, Vincente Minnelli, Rouben Mamoulian, etc., provides numerous examples.

In the narrative film the chief exponents of the moving camera were active during the fifties—George Sidney's *Scaramouche* (1952) contains model examples of how action can be concisely recorded by tracking; Hitchcock's *Rope* (1948), an essay in the single-camera/single-take film, took the 'roving spectator' concept to its ultimate conclusion. In Europe, Max Ophuls, disproving the widely-held belief that only in Hollywood can great technicians be found, contributed some of the most complex travelling shots ever made—the parallel track of car and boat in *La Signora di Tutti* (1934) through to the dazzling cinemascope movements in *Lola Montès* (1954). More recently, Alain Resnais used the tracking camera in the first person singular in *L'Année Dernière à Marienbad* (1961), and Jean-Luc Godard, having brought the hand-held moving camera back into vogue in *A Bout de Souffle* (1959), gave the ten-minute take a structural role in *Weekend* (1967).

In the independent cinema, sophisticated, studio-type moving camera-work is relatively rare. Ed Emshwiller (a professional cameraman) used rapid ground-level tracks in his *Relativity* (1966); Kenneth Anger, who enjoys a curious love–hate relationship with Hollywood, uses 'conventional' super-smooth tracks in *KKK* (1965) and *Scorpio Rising* (1963); and in a different vein, David Brooks' fluid hand-held camera movements are essential to the meaning of his films. But in many 'underground' films the informal movement of the camera and the informal editing (being intuitive) are so closely interconnected that it is impossible to discuss them separately.

Like the moving camera, experiments with special effects were mainly confined to the commercial cinema, being tailored to the narrative film, and only recently have they been open to avant-garde film-makers. Obviously Méliès takes the credit for suggesting the enormous 'magic' potential of the movie camera; his *La Danseuse Microscopique*, an effective use of double exposure using a black velvet background as a 'natural' matte, dates from 1902. In America *The Great Train Robbery* of a year later contains an early matte shot which allows a passing train to be seen through the telegraph office window. As with 'ghost shots', single-frame animations, etc., these effects were all created in-camera. Lescarboura, writing in 1920 in his book *Behind the Motion Picture Screen*, unconsciously hints at the way special effects were to develop: 'What cannot be done with the camera in the way of trick pictures, can be done in the laboratory by clever printing. Thus some of the most remarkable effects are the result of double or even triple printings in the making of the positives.'

The work of Norman O. Dawn, a special effects pioneer, points to the potential part to be played by the laboratories. Dawn perfected the 'glass shot' in which part of the camera's field of vision is replaced by a painted scene placed in front of the camera (plate 27) and enjoyed placing his actors in exotic settings matted together from as many as four different 'false' and 'real' elements (plate 28). At first he shot all the elements on location where they were liable to 'shift' if the camera moved; subsequently, he shot only the action on location and used a specially rigid studio camera for photographing his artwork. From Dawn's in-camera process it was only a small step for such re-exposure to take place in the printer, using a second strip of film to create the image.

With the coming of sound the advantages of containing all the action within the studio gave added strength to the special effects department. Of supreme importance was the development of the optical printer, which allowed the rephotographing of one strip of film (in the printer) on to another (in the process camera), one frame at a time. By varying the distance, position and movement of the process camera in relation to the printer head, a range of effects could be made that gave the operator almost as much freedom as an animator.

Having replaced most in-camera special effects, the optical printer was soon exploited to create exaggerated and fantastic forms—for their own effect. Simple dissolves and wipes gave way to a multiplicity of trick transitions (plate 29), in which one sequence spiralled, starred or even tore into the next. In *Flying Down to Rio* (1933), one apparently moving picture is folded off to reveal another. Lynn Dunn expresses contemporary enthusiasm for the process: 'Some of the effects are brainstorms, and one has to go almost into a trance to make them; and after they are finished it is hard to tell how they were done.'

The use of high-contrast film stocks in conjunction with the optical printer led to the development of more sophisticated travelling mattes, in which a moving photographic image replaced the still mask of Dawn's process (and its only alternative—the animated matte of the early live-action/animation cartoonists). This completely liberated the technique and led to a deluge of earthquakes, tidal waves and science-fiction monsters during the thirties (from the hands of James Basevi and others) that still provides Hollywood's one stable source of phantasmagoria.

Rear-screen projection also benefited from these new standards of printing, and often all exterior shots were relegated to the second unit. In MGM's *Captains Courageous* (1937), 'more than eighty per cent of the release footage was enacted before the process screen . . . and not one of the actors got nearer to the ocean than a Culver City sound stage'.

More than one technique could be used at a time. A contemporary reviewer of Merian Cooper's *King Kong* (1933) revealed that as well as Willis O'Brien's frame-by-frame animation of the sixteen-inch-high model ape, as many as six different trick processes were involved in some scenes; 'Dunning', 'Williams' and 'Pomeroy' transparency projection, miniatures, glass mattes and slow motion all combined together in the final printing.

For Cecil B. De Mille's *Cleopatra* (1934) Gordon Jennings created the illusion of a fleet of 'thirty-five or more' galleys engaged in battle—in fact there were only two 12-foot scale models. First he multiplied them by the 'old trick' of two parallel mirrors, then multiplied them again into two opposing fleets by split-screen double exposures. In close shots the same two models with cut-outs in the background were multiplied by optical printing. The result, though far from 'realistic', was closer in spirit to the kinetics of real conflict than many subsequent re-enactments have been.

In Europe no equivalent printing techniques were used until well into the forties. German cameramen preferred to make their effects in-camera. Ernst Lubitsch returned from a visit to Europe in 1933 and reported: 'In Europe, the optical printer is practically unknown . . . dissolves are made in the camera. Moreover, the cameramen there still have a great deal of trouble in doing this.' But he added that European editing devices were superior: 'Compared to those in use in Europe, the best of ours are crude and inconvenient.' The legacy of Eisenstein was still in force. (Eisenstein, significantly, had no time for special effects and largely avoided such 'distractions' as the moving camera.) UFA, however, did come up with one contribution to special-effects photography—the Schüfftan process, where actors were combined with scale models in front of the camera, the mirror surface that reflected the models being scraped away in parts to reveal the action. It was used successfully in Fritz Lang's *Metropolis* (1926) and was subsequently adopted in Hollywood.

Slavko Vorkapich, discussing the 'extremely few instances of the creative use of the motion-picture medium that exist', in an article 'Towards a true cinema' (*Film Culture*, no 19, 1959), is sensitive about the comparison of his montage with its Russian counterpart:

> If, with some hesitation, I mention some of my own work I can almost hear a few of them thinking: 'Now we know! You mean camera tricks! You mean montage: the Hollywood kind, not the Eisenstein kind! You mean flip-flops and wipes and zooms and the camera on the flying trapeze!'

He then emphasizes the need to distinguish 'beautiful photography'—a surface embellishment—and 'cinematography'—the 'gathering of visual-dynamic-meaningful elements, which creative cutting combines into living entities'. This recognition of the importance of kinetics provides a direct link with Eisenstein, but the cultural and political context in which Vorkapich and Eisenstein worked made other, more profound, differences inevitable. Eisenstein's montage was designed specifically to provoke thought and even direct action, while Vorkapich was commissioned to illustrate traumatic experiences in melodramas or to condense events important to the story that in any other form would take up too much time: for instance, Jeanette MacDonald's 'rise to fame' in *Maytime* (1937), and the outbreak of revolution in *Viva Villa* (1934). In *Crime without Passion* (1934), however, there is a sequence that suggests comparison with the final sequence of Eisenstein's *Strike*—Vorkapich's treatment of the shooting of the heroine, Margo, and the 'unleashing of the symbolic Furies':

Close-up: Margo's eyes staring at the gun (a frozen frame)
Dissolve to: close up of the muzzle of a gun, in exact overlap—the barrel being exactly where the eye-ball was
Close-up: the eye twitches, slightly
Close-up: the barrel of the gun; alternate black-and-white frames suggest the explosion
Close-up: Margo's eyes wince with pain
Close-up: (out of focus): smoke leaves the gun, a man's figure behind it
Mid-shot: Margo falls to the ground—slow motion

Close-up:	(before she hits the ground) a drop of blood strikes the floor; out of the drop of blood the Furies appear to rise and fly into the air—sailing out over the city.

(The Furies were shot stationary from vertically above, the camera approaching and passing them on its way down, to create the illusion of movement; plate 31.)

In the final sequence of *Strike*, Eisenstein dispenses with conventional continuity: the slaughter of a bull and the massacre of a crowd are intercut, their combination into one concept is entirely a mental process; the one visual link—the 'spilling of blood'—is itself conceptual. A purely visual link, such as Vorkapich's mimicry of the eye-ball by the gun barrel, would never occur in his work.

In this respect the Hollywood montage experts relate much more closely to Hans Richter's prologues of the twenties (see page 26). A sequence made by Vorkapich depicting the 'boom and bust of the twenties' for *The Conquerors* (1932), showing chimneys smoking, markets, the busy stock exchange, happy faces, stacks of coins piling higher and higher and then toppling, sad faces, etc., is strikingly similar to Hans Richter's *Inflation*. (Byron Haskin's montage on the end of prohibition and the Wall Street crash in *The Roaring Twenties* (1939), makes use of similar motifs, but adds an amusing optical shot of the 'canyon walls' of Wall Street symbolically 'melting' and collapsing.) What distinguishes Richter's work is his emphasis on an imposed overall rhythm.

During the period in which he was working for MGM, Vorkapich apparently attempted to persuade them to patronize experimental film work. He himself made two shorts—'pictorial interpretations' of Wagner's *Forest Murmurs* and Mendelssohn's *Fingal's Cave*—and managed to get MGM to buy the latter, but it was never shown publicly, being considered 'too artistic for general release'.

America since the war

No critic in pre-war America could have predicted the great burst of personal film-making that was to take place there during the late fifties and early sixties. The use of amateur cameras had been largely confined to the wealthy middle classes who had time for little other than the recreational use of their equipment. By the early fifties, however, film production equipment was becoming more accessible. During the war years the American armed forces had trained thousands of men as observers and had equipped them with 16-mm cameras; after the war most servicemen's rehabilitation programmes ('designed to fit them for civilian life') included a film appreciation course, introducing many of them to their first experience of committed cinema. Also, during the forties, the Motion Picture Foundation for Colleges and Universities was set up, a body largely sponsored by the film industry, which financially assisted and gave advice in the setting up of film workshops. Its first director, Professor Robert Gessner set out its intentions: 'to stimulate student production of 16-mm sound films'.

Until then there had been only three colleges in the entire United States where film could be studied (UCLA, USC and NYU). The rapid spread of television broadcasting provided further opportunities for film-work—locally—all over the country, and many personal film-makers gained access to equipment and supported themselves in this way (not least among them Stan Brakhage). As a transmitter of images, television also helped to de-sanctify film—removing it from its role of theatrical spectacle and demanding that it reflect and contribute to the domestic environment. Many films suffered from this change of role, but the result was a new, informal relationship with the image and a familiarity with techniques that was to influence the generation that grew up with television.

EAST COAST—CINEMA 16 AND THE GRYPHON GROUP

Hans Richter's move to the United States was prompted by the Nazi takeover in Germany. He was made director of the Institute of Film Techniques at City College, New York, which enabled him to resume his film-making almost as soon as he arrived. His first announced project was to shoot a story line to link together all his films, so they could be shown commercially at the World Theatre in New York. The money to do this was provided by Peggy Guggenheim. However, with the means available it now seemed more appropriate to start a completely new film, and Richter decided to make a collective work with his fellow emigrés Fernand Léger, Marcel Duchamp, Max Ernst, Man Ray and the American, Alexander Calder. The film, *Dreams that Money Can Buy* (1944–6), consists of six episodes: *The Girl with the Prefabricated Heart*—a love story between mannequins by Léger; a re-creation of *Rotoreliefs* and his *Nude Descending a Staircase* by Duchamp; a 'collage of nightmares' based on Ernst's series of five books within a book—*La Semaine de la Bonté*; a ballet based on Calder's mobiles; *Ruth Roses and Revolvers* by Man Ray; and Richter's own *Narcissus*, an allegory on the 'conflict between . . . inner life and reality'.

The film, nearly feature length, lacks the tight structure and visual impact of Richter's earlier work. He uses colour either realistically or to emphasize the symbolism, but never for its own sake as one might have hoped for in a work by artists so used to working with it. But the relatively leisurely pace of *Dreams* does provide a unique chance to see an informal side of the work of these major Dada artists—a side they rarely reveal. Continuing his role as chronicler of the Dada movement, Richter made *8* × *8* (1952–7), a series of incidents involving Duchamp, Arp, Cocteau and other celebrities (and some relatively unknowns), shot on location in Europe and America, using as a theme a game of chess. *Dadascope 1 and 2*, completed in 1957, were further anthologies, this time concentrating on sound—the sound of the chief Dada exponents making poetry, reading their works. The images are almost subservient, leitmotifs of Richter's from the twenties—the revolving eyes—camera tricks—intercut with portraits from the present and past: portraits of artists and portraits of his own films.

Richter contributed more to the American cinema than just his films. His presence as a lecturer and writer gave the new generation of independent film-makers a personal link with the major achievements of the European avant-garde of the twenties.

The first American to reach a wide audience with 'personal' films was Maya Deren. She pioneered a dynamic approach to the screening of films by the film-makers themselves that led to a complete restructuring of non-theatrical distribution in the United States.

Maya Deren made six films in her lifetime, five of them during the period 1943–8. (Her last, *The Very Eye of Night*, was completed in 1959, only two years before her death.) Her first film, *Meshes of the Afternoon* (1943), was made in Los Angeles with Alexander Hammid, the noted documentary film-maker, who was then her husband. In it she plays a girl who is finally driven to suicide by her obsessive, subconscious reaction to a number of half-dreamed incidents. A knife, seen first lying on a table, repeatedly confronts her until she allows herself to 'submit' and be killed by it. In structure the film is close to the French Surrealist genre, but Deren replaces the deliberately arbitrary treatment of time and location that characterizes Surrealist works with a precisely calculated technique. She likes, for example, to show the true proportions of a room, then to stretch a person's movement across it by the use of slow motion and repeat shots subtly disguised in the editing. By establishing a continuity of camera movement she achieves a double shock from an unexpected move between one location and another. In the outline of a part of *At Land* (1944) that follows, these transitions are indicated by a stroke (/):

> Waves (partly in reverse motion) wash ashore a limp body—a girl's body. Becoming alive, she crawls up the sloping sand/ presses through thick foliage/crawls along a table top (people seated on either side, as if at a banquet, talk animatedly without noticing her). At the far end a chess game is in progress. She becomes a player. The pieces move themselves. A piece falls off/into a rock pool/is swept down over smooth rocks to the sea. She follows it, hesitantly . . .

In *A Study in Choreography for Camera* (1945), the first of her dance films, Deren concentrates entirely upon the continuity of camera movement which becomes the main subject of the film. Talley Beatty, the dancer, begins a step—the lowering of his extended leg—in an open wood space, and completes it, apparently in the same shot, in an enclosed room. His dance takes him through as many changes of location as of movement. In *Meditation on Violence* (1948), a dance poem based on Chinese boxing, the dance is the camera's as it watches the boxer; it then becomes the opponent and dodges the boxer's blows. Deren explains (in *Film Culture* 29) that an essential part of Woo Tang boxing is that 'it never extends movement to the extreme—but always rounds it about . . . No movement is ever concluded, it merely leads again. That makes it metaphoric, dynamic, the very principle of life itself.' The film's form is deliberately without climax—the whole of the last part runs backwards—but so well balanced are the movements, so well 'rounded about', that this reversal is accepted as quite natural; again—'the basic principle of life is that the dynamic was the functional flow of negative and positive, repeated'.

In her writing, Maya Deren demands the right for objects and actions to be seen as representing only themselves, and rejects all inference of symbolism in her work. Her monograph, *An Anagram of Ideas on Art Form and Film* (published in 1946 by Alicat Bookshop Press), provided one of the most complete statements by any film-artist of their total position until the publication of Brakhage's *Metaphors on Vision* in 1963. All her recorded statements convey a complete confidence in the validity of her position as a personal film-maker that undoubtedly inspired many young Americans to follow her example. Unable to place her films with a commercial distributor, she hired them out herself from her home in New York. Early in 1946 she rented the Provincetown Playhouse on MacDougal Street, New York, for a one-night show of her first three films (this story has become almost apocryphal). They generated such an interest that repeat screenings were arranged at once. This sudden success led to a whole series of performances all over the States, a highspot being their showing at the Film as Art series in San Francisco.

Deren's success also encouraged Amos Vogel to start using the Provincetown Playhouse as a base for his 'Cinema 16', a club that set out to show 'outstanding social documentaries, controversial adult screen fare, advanced experimental films, classics of the international cinema and medical-psychiatric studies', developing in 1950 an additional distribution outlet that handled an extraordinary cross-section of films, ranging from Deren and Brakhage through Franju and Antonioni to the documentaries of Paul Rotha. As a showcase for experimental films, Cinema 16 was unchallenged. Deren and Vogel together formed the Creative Film Foundation to promote and assist experimental film-makers in their work. But Vogel's insistence upon his personal selection of all Cinema 16 programmes led to ill feeling among certain film-makers. According to Willard Maas, it was Vogel's continued refusal to show or distribute the films of Marie Menken (Maas's wife) that finally persuaded the Gryphon Group to act as producer/distributor; later, his refusal to distribute Brakhage's *Anticipation of the Night* (1958) was to be a contributory reason for the creation of the New York Film-makers Co-operative.

The Gryphon Group was a pioneer attempt at collective film production. With Maas and Menken as prime movers, and Norman McLaren briefly involved, their first work was *Geography of the Body* (1943), a series of close-ups of a (collective) body photographed through magnifying glasses, set to a poetic commentary. It was photographed largely by Menken and directed by Maas.

Thereafter, Maas made a series of psychodramas based on quasi-homosexual themes, assisted on the first, *Images in the Snow* (1943–8), by Marie Menken, and on the later ones, *The Mechanics of Love* (1955) and *Narcissus*, by Ben Moore.

Marie Menken has always worked very much on her own. Her *Visual Variations on Noguchi* (1945) was originally made in response to a request from the Merce Cunningham/John Cage partnership for a movie background to their ballet *The Seasons*. (As Stan Vanderbeek's series of film loops was made some twenty years later for the Cunningham/Cage *Variation 5*.) In it Noguchi's abstract sculpture spins and floats as if it were made weightless by the buoyancy of the camerawork. Menken made no more films until 1957, when in *Glimpse of the Garden*, a very childlike study of trees, paths and flowers, she announced her return to the medium. Each of her subsequent movies seems to have been prompted by one simple idea or situation, and she adapts her style accordingly. *Arabesque for Kenneth Anger* (1961), for example, records details of the Moorish Palace, the Alhambra, Granada, and was made 'as a thank you to Kenneth for helping me with my shooting'. The earlier *Hurry Hurry* (1957) combined scientific footage of sperms thrashing about (frustratingly never getting anywhere) with a light superimposition of a close-up of flames. *Go Go Go* (1962–4)—a film she herself is particularly fond of—is a portrait of New York, sometimes shot in single frames to condense and clarify the movements of the city. Similarly, *Wrestling* (1964), her only recent work to have been seen in Europe to date, condenses several bouts of television wrestling into five minutes of flickering action, making the camera's movements almost as nervous as the image itself.

The simplicity and integrity of her work has greatly endeared Marie Menken to the younger generation of New York film-makers, and she has appeared recently in a number of their films.

During the early sixties, the Gryphon Group's productions included work by Stan Brakhage, Charles Boultenhouse, Gregory Markopoulos, Ben Moore, Charles Henry Ford in addition to Maas and Menken. Then, almost at its height, the group was eclipsed by the newly-formed New York Film-Maker's Co-operative.

WEST COAST—THE ART IN CINEMA SERIES

Immediate post-war film production on the West Coast of America found a focal centre in the Art in Cinema series of film screenings and symposiums started in San Francisco in 1947 by Frank Stauffacher and Richard Foster. The published programme that accompanied the first season at the San Francisco Museum of Art took the form of a (non-profit-making) book, *Art in Cinema*, a collection of statements on the nature of the 'art film' by its leading American and European exponents, with a chronological series of filmographies, a history of the avant-garde compiled by Hans Richter, and a large number of stills.

Of the contemporary film-artists mentioned in the text, Mary Ellen Bute, Maya Deren, Dwinell Grant, Douglas Crockwell and Hans Richter represent the East Coast, and John and James Whitney, James Broughton and Sidney Peterson and Oskar Fischinger represent the West Coast. Other West Coast film-makers who had already made films of merit, Kenneth Anger, Curtis Harrington, Harry Smith, closely followed by Jordan Belson and Gregory Markopoulos, were included later in the series.

Many West Coast film-makers have boasted that their work represents the most complete break with previous film-making traditions, yet in the West Coast abstract school of film-making there is more obvious continuity with past achievements than anywhere else in current American cinema. Eggeling, who created the first truly abstract films, would certainly recognize his descendants in the Whitney brothers, Jordan Belson and John Stehura, for while Belson, for example, would prefer to regard his films as metaphysical rather than abstract, he shares with Eggeling the demand that the experience of his film be recognized in visual terms alone. (Or, more correctly, in audio-visual terms since sound is very much an integral part of his movies.) No immediate reference is made to existing recognizable phenomena. A direct link between Europe of the twenties and the West Coast was the presence in Hollywood from 1935 of Oskar Fischinger, his influence being later reinforced by Stauffacher's retrospective of the early work of Eggeling and Richter.

Oskar Fischinger started making films in Germany in 1921, but nothing survives of the *Studies* he produced before 1928. In 1926 he went to Berlin and worked on special effects sequences for Fritz Lang's *Frau im Mond*. In 1929 he was involved in the animation of a section of Ruttman's *Melody of the World*, then started on his own surviving *Studies 5 to 12*, a series of black and white abstract animations mostly set to light classical music. In 1933 he produced his famous *Circles*, the first Gasparcolour film (a process he helped to perfect), and *Composition in Blue* (plate 33), which won a prize at Venice and led to his being invited to Hollywood by Paramount. These two films were not only his first in colour; they also marked a change in technique from the earlier drawings to paper cut-outs and even three-dimensional forms filmed in depth (the coloured blocks in vertical and horizontal stacks in *Composition*). While still in Germany, he produced his first commercials including the Muratti Cigarette advertisement, in which lines of cigarettes march like soldiers—a technique that Ray and Charles Eames were to develop, for instance, in *Toccata for Toy Trains*.

From 1936 Fischinger worked in Hollywood, producing another jazz composition *Allegretto* in that year, and two further colour compositions—*Optical Poem* for MGM in 1937/8 to music by Liszt, and *An American March* (1940) to *Stars and Stripes* by Sousa.

Ironically, Hollywood was unable to support Fischinger's talent; the one commission he received that could have led to a wider acceptance of his work—the sequence he designed for Disney's *Fantasia* (1940) based on Bach's *Toccata and Fugue*—was rejected as being 'too abstract' and replaced by an inferior section that almost parodies his style. Thereafter, his output rapidly declined; he undertook a few commercial projects—*Muntz TV* (1953), *Oklahoma* (1954), etc., but largely concentrated on painting as an activity. His final major work as a film-artist—*Motion Painting No 1* (1949; plate 34)—already reflects this change. A new technique (the very complex movements in the film are entirely the result of manipulating paint on glass) was paralleled by a new source of finance—the Guggenheim Foundation. Hollywood had thus (almost symbolically) declared its hand—in future the production of experimental work would have to be the concern of philanthropists or the film-makers themselves. Only in the sixties, when the 'underground' became a serious critical box-office attraction, did the studios begin to reconsider their position.

The lesson implicit in Hollywood's treatment of Fischinger is reinforced by the experiences of Mary Ellen Bute, whose films in some ways closely resemble Fischinger's. They are concerned with the movement of abstract shapes to musical accompaniment. Her first solo works, *Anitra's Dance* and *Rhythm in Light* (both 1936), coincide almost exactly with Fischinger's arrival in Hollywood. However, Bute worked quite outside the studio framework, her husband, Ted Nemeth, acting as her producer.

Having worked with Schillinger and Lewis Jacobs on their *Synchronization* in 1934, she appears to have adopted Schillinger's mathematical system in the composition of visuals and sound in most of her early films—in contrast to Fischinger's more personal and subjective use of rhythm. Using two- and three-dimensional everyday objects in extreme close-up, shot through long- and short-focus lenses, using fragments of mirrors, distorting lenses, prisms, even shooting through ice cubes for effect, she constructed her movies with a sense of the theatrical, accentuated by dramatic lighting, which proved very popular with audiences.

Mary Ellen Bute made two or three films a year between 1936 and 1941, then apparently ceased production until the early fifties. In the later series—*Polka-Graph* (1953), *Abstronics* (1954) and *Colour Rhapsody* (variously dated 1954 and 1958)—she utilized electronic images, filming oscilloscope patterns, superimposing them through colour filters, etc., but still composing in counterpoint to the sound-track and leaving the exploitation of the full potential of the cathode ray tube to the next generation of film-makers.

Very little has been written about the early work of Mary Ellen Bute[1]—it rarely appears in retrospectives of experimental films and is apparently unavailable to film societies.

Though working independently, her films were made to be seen commercially and, for a time, some of them were included in the pre-feature spectacular at Radio City Music Hall in New York. With Fischinger she was perhaps the last of the generation of experimental film-makers who worked on 35-mm film in the expectation of commercial patronage. Thereafter, film-makers began to realize that distribution and exhibition would also have to become part of their concern. Feeling it more important to reach a large audience, Bute and Nemeth have more recently turned to feature production in the more widely accepted narrative ninety-minute format. *The Boy who saw Through* (1956–8) was followed by *Passages from Finnegans Wake* (1964–5), which contains a few moments of subliminal rapid-cutting, but is not distinguished otherwise.

Also involved in 'experimental' animation in the forties was Douglas Crockwell, whose early attempts with oil-on-glass techniques may have been known to Fischinger. Crockwell's work is completely 'amateur'—he was an illustrator by profession and had no commercial stake in movies. He experimented only because of his interest in the 'evolution of abstract forms as directed by free association'. His own description of the method used in *Glen Falls Sequence* (1946) (in *Art in Cinema* 1947) is typically modest:

> I set up an animation easel with the camera mounted overhead and the work area arranged much as a draughtsman's desk,

[1] Illustrated by the confusion over the title of a film she made in 1940 (apparently animated by McLaren) called *Spool's Sport* in *Art in Cinema*, *Sport Spools* in Lewis Jacob's *The Rise of the American Film* and *Spook Sport* (most appropriate as it seems to have been about ghosts) in Robert Benayoun's *Le Dessin Animé après Walt Disney*.

> except that the working area consisted of several movable layers of glass slightly separated. The basic idea was to paint continuing pictures on these various layers with plastic paint, adding at times and removing at times, and to a certain extent these early attempts were successful. The basic process was changed from time to time with varying results and I have still made no attempt yet to stabilize the method. Somewhat as a consequence of this has been the fragmentary character of the work produced.

In fact, the technique of his first *Fantasmagoria* series (1938–40), which was similar, was later improved by the use of non-drying oil paint on the back of the glass sheets (as in *The Chase* 1940), then further sophisticated by air brush and pantograph.

In an article in *Film Culture* 32, 'A background to free animation', Crockwell records that he initially contemplated doing a series of 'key' drawings and employing a studio to do the fill-ins, but realized that the 'free-flowing forms' that he achieved with his slow-speed photography and manipulation of paint were beyond the resources of 'jerky' Hollywood animation.

The 'fragmentary character' he refers to gives his work an extraordinarily contemporary appearance—it has many affinities with the non-sequentially developed 'head drawings' of the psychedelic sixties. In *Glen Falls Sequence*, recognizable symbols —a crucifix, a table, human heads (one gives birth to another), 'surreal' landscapes—are intermixed with three-dimensional objects—phallic shapes, egg shapes, random paper cut-outs, a Fischinger-like play of rectangles, pixillated pills on a smooth background and so on—mutating and suddenly jumping with considerably more free association than either Buñuel and/or Dali films achieved. For *Long Bodies* (1946–7), Crockwell invented an entirely new technique, and one that at least in cinematic terms is more aesthetically integrated:

> A three-dimensional block (3 × 4 in.) any length, is thoughtfully built up of many pieces of colored wax interlaced and twisted to form a progressing composition. The end of the block is successively sliced off and photographed. The resultant animation is delightfully fluid and unique. If some of the waxes are transparent or translucent the motion becomes strangely anticipatory and unworldly. This is a controllable medium with untouched potentials.[1]

[1] 'A background to free animation' *Film Culture* 32.

The 'potential' was only to be fully exploited some twenty years later, when exactly the same technique was rediscovered for use in medicine, in this case whole organs being solidified with plastic material, then sliced and photographed successively to give an illusion of travelling through a complete brain.

John and James Whitney began making animated abstract films in 1941. Starting, in their *Variations* series (1941–3), with the movement of geometric and curvilinear forms, using scaled-down drawings in a technique quite similar to Fischinger's; they improved it by devising a method of graphically composing and recording synthetic sound to closely relate to the image:

> The principle resembles less a musical instrument than certain devices used for charting the rise and fall of ocean waves. Pendulums instead of waves create the ebb and flow movement. This motion is greatly demagnified and registered on the narrow space of the motion picture film provided for the soundtrack . . . The patterns themselves generate tones in the sound projector. The instrument has a selection of some thirty pendulums adjusted in frequency relationship to each other so as to form a scale. They can be swung singly or in any combination.[1]

Apart from being able to score the soundtrack to within a fraction of a frame, the Whitneys were pleased to find that 'the quality of the sound evokes no image distraction as was found in other music'.

Entering their next series of films at the Brussels Experimental Film Festival in 1949 under the collective title of *Five Abstract Film Exercises, Studies in Motion*, they were awarded a special prize in recognition of their achievement with sound.

In the last years of the forties, John produced a series of films set to (existing) musical compositions, using a combination of earlier paper cut-out techniques with patterns created by the diffraction of light in an oil bath, the design being caused by a stylus 'etching' the surface of the oil.

Thereafter the brothers worked separately, James taking almost fifteen years to complete just two films, one eight minutes long, the other ten minutes; while John involved himself in a continuous exploration of the graphic potential of first the analogue, then the digital computer. Until the mid-sixties, most of John's output was for commercial projects, including the credit sequence of Hitchcock's *Vertigo* (1958) (in association with arch-titler Saul Bass) and a multiscreen collaboration with Charles Eames for an

[1] 'Audio-visual music' by John and James Whitney, *Art in Cinema* 1947.

exhibition in Moscow in 1957, and this led to his setting up the Motion Graphics Inc. in 1960, a commercial firm to handle his commissioned work.

The full range of his analogue work in the fifties is demonstrated in *Catalogue* (1961), a collection of brilliantly coloured ever-changing line, dot and letter patterns that spiral, expand and contract with a remarkably 'natural', though, to the lay eye at least, unpredictable movement. As a catalogue, the film has no unifying structure, a part of its purpose being to record a number of techniques, yet the 'completeness' of the computer's action gives the film a visual authority that makes it compelling viewing. *Permutations* (1968), made using the increased sophistication of the digital computer, in fact appears much more mechanical. Using a series of basic dot patterns (basic to the design—mathematically doubtless they are very complex) generated and evolved by the computer, Whitney then elaborated them on film, editing and combining images, rephotographing and printing them on the optical printer through coloured filters, until he arrived at the succession of images that together satisfied him. The principle involved in the latter part of this process has been the one constant factor in the Whitneys' technique through all their movies. At present no computer seems capable of keeping pace with the artist's evolving aesthetic criteria, during its action. The procedure is quite distinct; the artist makes an initial speculation or instruction which the computer follows and develops; then the artist combines and reassembles the material. In the analogue work the images are composed frame by frame, a technique much closer to conventional animation, and a reason perhaps for the greater stylistic unity apparent in the earlier films. James Whitney's *Yantra* (1950–7) apparently made no use of the computer at all, the basic dot structures being drawn by hand on cards before being multiplied, coloured and spun into patterns in the optical printer (plate 35). *Yantra* comes closer to being a 'pure abstract' film than any other I know—abstract in the sense that it keeps the audience's attention completely, yet leaves the mind totally free from preconception and association. It is an object of meditation that requires no aesthetic or spiritual instruction to be appreciated. In *Lapis* (1963–6), James Whitney shortened his creative process by making use of a simpler version of his brother's analogue computer. Again the completed film has a spiritual unity quite unlike any other. The dots spin out, collide and form one stunning configuration after another; a series of lap dissolves leads from one image straight into another; the film has a governing visual rhythm as vital as that of human breathing. Together the Whitney brothers have demonstrated that the apparently cold world of mathematical calculations can apply its resources to meeting essential human aesthetic and spiritual needs.

Jordan Belson is a close friend of James Whitney; his films, with Whitney's, form the finest achievement of non-objective cinema to date. Belson's interest in film was stimulated by the Film as Art series, where he was particularly struck by the films of Hans Richter and Oskar Fischinger. Like Richter, his first films, *Transmutation* (1947) and *Improvisations No 1* (1948), were made directly from painted scrolls, each strip being divided into 'frames' which were photographed in succession. The images were already non-objective, but related to biological phenomena. Of these films, only the scrolls themselves survive.

Belson returned to painting until 1952 when he began a series of single-frame animations that included: *Bop Scotch* (1952–3), a textural film of close-ups of paving stones, man-hole covers, mosaics, water, painted brick walls, etc., set to a lively jazz track; *Mandala* (1952), in which animated circles fluctuate in size and mutate in rhythmic cycles at close to heart-beat rate (prefiguring things to come); and *LSD* (1954), in which he indicated something of the visions induced by the drug.

Between 1957 and 1960 Belson worked on the *Vortex Concerts*, one of the most interesting series of 'expanded media' events ever devised. Held at the Morrison Planetarium in San Francisco, Belson has described them as 'a new form of theatre based on the combination of electronics, optics and architecture . . . a pure theatre appealing directly to the senses'. Using the dome of the planetarium as a vast screen, Belson made use of specially-prepared films and light-sources to compose on an unprecedented scale. Most of his numerous projectors were modified in some way—some could zoom, some had kaleidoscope lenses, some had irises fitted in front of the lens and could act as a movable mask, many could rotate on their axes; a strobe was present to add a flicker if required, still (slide) projectors provided large areas of colour, grids, etc.; the images were almost entirely non-objective, but very closely related to the music of the performances—the responsibility of Henry Jacobs. Jacobs had equally expanded the 'normal' concept of musical performance. The works were mainly electronic (Stockhausen, Mayusumi, Badings, etc.) and were played through forty speakers located round the perimeter of the dome and in the middle of the floor. A keyboard made possible the 'playing' of the speakers so that sound could be made to come from one direction, every direction or in sequence around the dome.

Both Belson and Jacobs believed that their work related closely to states in the subconscious mind and to basic psychological and physiological phenomena. The flooding rhythms of sound and the geometric star patterns of light they equated to basic stimuli potentially present in the consciousness when 'not blocked by repression'.

The *Vortex Concerts* were immensely popular and influential. They certainly contributed to the West Coast obsession with 'subliminal' imagery in light-shows and films, but more in particular, the success of their presentation at the Brussels World Fair in 1958 undoubtedly encouraged the great number of 'multi-screen' presentations at subsequent Expo-type occasions. Unfortunately, nothing attempted by others in this field, including the Eames team, Francis Thompson, Don Levy, etc., has matched either the ambition or the achievement of Belson and Jacobs.

During the *Vortex* period, Belson made *Flight* (1958), *Raga* (1959) and *Seance* (1959). The *Vortex Concerts* were ended in 1960 when the Planetarium decided they could no longer afford the spare time. No other suitable home could be found. The films Belson has made since then are the only ones he considers still worthy of attention. Into them he has concentrated the sum of all his visual experience plus his deep spiritual searching. Made on the 'optical bench' (a construction of his own design which combines the essential workings of an animation rostrum with the techniques of 'live' photography), the visual complexity of these works—*Allures* (1961), *Re-Entry* (1964), *Phenomena* (1965), *Samadhi* (1967) and *Momentum* (1968–9)—defy verbal description. The image source is 'cosmic' rather than 'terrestial'—suns, stars, points of light, aurora, nebulae, etc.—although brief reminders of 'earth culture' appear—a man and a woman seen through a barrage of lights and distortions on television, then a fragment of German *Lieder* in *Phenomena*, a rocket ship blasting off in *Momentum*.

Allures, the most mathematically-structured of the series, is thematically linked to the concept of 'cosmogenesis'—the perpetual rebirth of matter at *all* levels from the molecular to the galactic. *Re-Entry* creates an analogy between space flight (lift-off voyage and re-entry—John Glenn had just made his solo flight) and the progress of the soul from death through a period of suspension to rebirth, as described in the *Bardo Thodol* (the *Tibetan Book of the Dead*). The re-entry of the title exists on two levels, one contained within the images of the film, the other being the return of the viewer to 'normal' consciousness and perception after the film is over.

The physical presence of Belson's films is overwhelming. It is as if he had allowed his camera to run uninterrupted for a few minutes in front of some previously undiscovered phenomenon;

he insists that he cannot create any of his effects until he has discovered them in reality for himself. His 'suns' and 'clouds' are as real as those recorded by the *camera obscura*; but he scrupulously rejects any images that make the process of their creation in any way apparent. Belson has no wish to distract the viewer with reminders of the 'twenty-four-frames-per-second' nature of what they are watching.

Samadhi came after a period of intense Yoga discipline. In Sanskrit, *Samadhi* means 'that state of consciousness in which the individual soul merges with the universal soul'. The film is structured by the sound of controlled breathing—the image flow is punctuated by periods during which the screen grows increasingly lighter till a brilliant yellowish white predominates. This phenomenon relates to the 'tattric lights' that accompany the flow of energy to the 'chakras'—the nerve centres along the spinal column and in the head.

Momentum is a serene (after the forceful impact of *Samadhi*) progress of images (some made with videotape and computer assistance) that represents a physical/spiritual journey to the sun. A rocket blasts off and passes through the clouds. Through a series of lap dissolves the sun is approached and reveals itself and the structure of its continual evolution. From the solar winds and prominences of the surface the viewer travels through to the central atom, to its nucleus, and through again to a level where the fusion of the atom and the creation of a new star are seen as one event.

Belson is certainly one of the finest film-artists alive—yet his works are relatively unknown. Throughout the period of the evolution of the film co-operatives in America, he held out for the kind of recognition from the film industry that Vorkapich and Fischinger had sought, believing that the exhibition conditions and returns to the film-maker offered by the co-ops were detrimental and inadequate. He sold his first works to Pike at the Creative Film Society; then, after a long period of waiting, he was at last offered acceptable amounts (for his recent works) by the American Film Institute and by Universal's Education and Visual Arts Division. He has supported himself on occasions by doing special effects work for Hollywood, his most recent contribution being for *Doppelgänger* (*Journey to the Far Side of the Sun* 1968–9).

When Dick Foster left Frank Stauffacher and the Art in Cinema Society, his position was taken over by Harry Smith, whose first achievement was to arrange the screening of the early works of Kenneth Anger. His own work, however, remained relatively unknown until Jonas Mekas arranged for their exhibition in New

York in the mid-sixties. Despite the fact that Smith has been making important animations since 1939, none of the histories of the subject even mention his name.

His first works, dating from the period 1939 to 1946, were made by hand drawing, batiking or etching directly on to the film stock. Smith was greatly disappointed to learn from Stauffacher that Len Lye had already made direct films, but the originality of his work and his application (*Number 3*—a film of batiked squares—took five years to complete) far exceed Lye's English films.

The Film as Art series brought Smith into contact with the Whitney brothers and Oskar Fischinger, and *Numbers 4* and *5*, the last of the direct films, show something of Fischinger's influence. *Number 4* begins with a shot of a painting in which each stroke represents a particular note in a tune by Dizzie Gillespie—*Manteca*; *Number 5—Circular Tensions*—is dedicated to Fischinger. Around 1950 (all dates are obscure in Smith's biography), the Guggenheim Foundation gave him money to make a series of optically printed studies, including a three-dimensional experiment, based on an extension of his earlier work. After another break of almost six years Smith went to New York where he began the 'alchemical labours' that many consider to be his greatest works. *Number 10* (a study for *Number 11*) is an 'exposition of Buddhism and the Kaballa in the form of a collage'. The all-over density of its coloured mandala-like images, and the increasing number of mutations that they undergo, make it one of the most complex and fascinating animations that exist. But it is the simpler, black-and-white *Number 12* (plate 37) that Smith's followers find the most rewarding. This film, *Heaven and Earth Magic* or the *Magic Feature*, was originally over six hours long (it now runs for an hour) and was incomplete even at that length. Simple cut-out pictures of objects perform together in a plot directed by Smith's interpretation of the Surrealist principle of 'psychic automatism'. Initially, Smith 'filed' all his collected objects according to subject—then built up all the possible permutations. 'Say there's a hammer in it and there's a vase and there's a woman and there's a dog. Various things could be done —hammer hits dog; woman hits dog; dog jumps into vase; so forth . . .' But despite the deliberate exclusion of conscious choice, the end product appears far from arbitrary—an awful logic seemingly governs all the events.

As with many of Smith's works, *Number 12* was originally intended to be projected with an additional visual overlay, in this case the projection of a series of static slides of the participatory objects from the film, which were to appear according to the response of the audience.

Number 13 was an abortive attempt to make a commercial film of his own version of events in the Land of Oz, and though he got as far as running tests on the enormous multiplane camera he had built, it was never completed.

Number 14 (*Late Superimpositions*) marked a complete break in style, being a superimposition work using 'Mr Fleischman's butcher shop in New York and the Kiowa [Indians] around Anadarko, Oklahoma with cognate material' as its subject.

Though he cannot claim to have invented all his techniques, Harry Smith certainly discovered them in ways no others have. The cut-out technique of *Numbers 10*, *11* and *12* has been re-created in turn by animators as diverse as Jan Lenica, Norman Rubington, Stan Vanderbeek and Larry Jordan, each developing his own particular style and meaning; but none has equalled the extraordinary authority of Smith's achievement.

Developing concurrently with the West Coast abstract school, was a movement that had its roots more in Maya Deren's work than in Richter's or Fischinger's. In San Francisco, James Broughton and Sidney Peterson led the field; in Los Angeles, Curtis Harrington and Kenneth Anger. The aspect of Deren's work that these film-makers took as their point of departure was her use of personal fantasy—which contained the seeds of both film poetry and the psychodrama.

James Broughton's work embodied the late forties' and early fifties' concept of the poetic role of the film-maker. On his first two films—*Mother's Day* (1948) and *The Adventures of Jimmy* (1950)—he was assisted by Kermit Sheets and used Frank Stauffacher as cameraman. In *Jimmy* (plate 38), he himself plays the principal role of the 'child of the backwoods who discovers the confusion and pressures of the metropolis'. 'Stalked by ladies', he tries psychoanalysis and prayer as a solution, lives in slums, 'exhausts himself in dance-halls' and returns somehow to his cabin surrounded by a harem. In *Loony Tom the Happy Lover* (1951), Kermit Sheets takes the part of a similarly naïve character, dressed in Chaplinesque baggy trousers and bowler hat, who 'prances around the country making outrageous love to every woman he encounters'.

Broughton's translation of the drama of existence into an allegory of the intuitive poet's conflict with the absurdities of reality, is a theme comparable to Cocteau's (for instance, in *Le Sang d'un Poète*). Both film-makers are able to make the most illustrative action appear lyrical, but Broughton, fortunately, shares none of Cocteau's preoccupation with mythology. Instead, he adopts the comic posture of Keystone: 'I wanted to capture the delight in movement and inventive action which existed in the early cinema, but with a certain marked and poetic difference.'

Four in the Afternoon (1951), a setting of four of Broughton's own poems, marks the beginning of a more whimsical style which reached its height in *The Pleasure Garden* (1953), a semi-commercial film he made in the grounds of the Crystal Palace, London. It was his last film for nearly fourteen years.

With less literary involvement in poetry, but film-poets none the less, Sidney Peterson and Hy Hirsh collaborated in 1947 on *The Cage, Clinic of Stumble* and the *Horror Dream* (the last also with John Cage). Peterson taught at the California School of Fine Arts and made most of his films there, his subjects and styling leaning towards the surrealistic. *Lead Shoes* (1949), probably his best-known work, centres around a game of hopscotch, drawn out and played in reverse, and a woman's awkward attempt to revive a man in a diving suit. The fragmented presentation of the sequences and soundtrack combined with the alternate expansion and squeezing of the images (by use of an anamorphic lens) gives the piece an almost psychotic atmosphere. This formal use of distortion gave the 'subjective shot' a completely new role. Instead of using effects to imitate reality, film-makers distorted reality to equate with a subjective vision.

After working with Peterson in California, Hy Hirsh left for Europe where he worked alternately in Paris and Amsterdam. There he developed in complete isolation a graphic cinema that extended the lyrical photography of Ralph Steiner's films, and which at the same time relates closely to the recent work of O'Neill, Strand, etc., in Los Angeles. *Autumn Spectrum* and *Défense d'Afficher* make rhythmic abstractions of their subjects—the reflections in the canals of Amsterdam and the tattered posters on the billboards of Paris. *Come Closer* converts oscilloscope-created images into neon-like circles that rotate, overlap and fade into each other in front of highly coloured backgrounds. (The effect was increased initially by use of a three-dimensional process.) With his last film, *La Couleur de la Forme*, Hirsh demonstrated his mastery of the optical printer by creating an optical rhyme (as in Richter's *Two Pence Magic*), in which the images reverse colour and motion in a series of almost subliminal overlaps.

Due to his self-imposed exile, Hy Hirsh has never received the recognition due to him; his films are hardly ever shown in New York and almost no articles have been written about him. He suffered (he is dead now) the consequences of being in the wrong place at the wrong time.

The early films of Kenneth Anger, Curtis Harrington, Gregory Markopoulos and Stan Brakhage provided the first manifestation of a new sensibility that arose during the late forties and early fifties and probably constitutes America's first completely original contribution to the avant-garde film. No film-makers in the past had been prepared to probe as deeply or as specifically into the workings of their own subconscious; 'personal' subjects had been dealt with in the acceptable terms of 'universal experience', or were clothed in the redeeming guise of allegory and symbolic action (*Le Sang d'un Poète*, *Lot in Sodom*, etc.). These film-makers, while not discarding either form, invested their work with an intensely personal vision that demanded a sympathetic emotional response from the audience. Their technique, although no less inventive, appears raw beside earlier avant-garde expressions, the beauty of the films lying in emotional integrity rather than photographic elegance. Jonas Mekas wrote:

> In American experimental-poetic films, Stan Brakhage or Kenneth Anger could serve as an example of the kind of modern film-poet who creates, not according to the technical rules of film-making (à la Spottiswoode) but rather according to the rules of his own subconscious—that is where the real creation begins. And only with the cinema-sense established at that depth can we hope for the art of cinema to emerge.[1]

In the case of Anger, Harrington, Markopoulos and Brakhage, the psychodrama served as a vehicle for only a brief initial period, before the emergence of a mature style. This pattern has been followed by many other young film-makers—as though it were necessary to make an emotional commitment to the medium before being allowed to master it.

Kenneth Anger and Curtis Harrington both began making films in earnest during the early forties, Harrington on 8mm, Anger on 16mm. When the Art in Cinema series gave them an opportunity to exhibit their work, Harrington chose to show *Fragment of Seeking* (1946) and Anger his *Fireworks* (1947). Both films deal explicitly with homosexual experience, and in each case the film-maker himself played the central character. Harrington's film (plate 40) concerns a young man who, tortured by his own narcissism, attempts to respond to a girl who offers herself to him but finds she is no more to him than a mockingly blonde-wigged skele-

[1] 'Experiment in the Fifties', *Film Book 1* 1959.

ton. Anger, aged seventeen at the time, plays the 'dreamer' in his film, who 'goes out in the night seeking "a light" ', directly confronting the frustrated fantasies of his waking life. The 'light' is a triple symbol, representing the classic pick-up phrase, his initiation, and the match that sets light to the phallic Roman candle of the title. It still rates as one of the most powerful films ever made.

Harrington continued to produce his quieter, though none the less 'authentic' films with *Picnic* (1948), a satire on middle-class emotions, and *On the Edge* (1949; plate 39), in which a man attempts to go out into the world but cannot cut the thread that attaches him to his mother. During the fifties he turned to mythological subjects (as did both Anger and Markopoulos) to make *Dangerous Houses* (1952), an interpretation of Odysseus' encounter with Circe and his descent into Hades, and *Wormwood Star* (1953), 'in which the painter Cameron and her work are presented; achieving an alchemical transmutation'. (He started to direct 'commercial' features in 1961 with *Night Tide*.)

Kenneth Anger's contribution to the American experimental film has been enormous, but his position is a curious one. While the subjects of his films have become almost synonymous with the 'underground' (not necessarily with his approval), his technical approach to film-making is often closer to Hollywood (at Hollywood's most ambitious). This apparent conservatism has certainly contributed to the popularity of his work, at the same time emphasizing the originality of the subjects.

Anger's childhood was spent in Hollywood; he appeared, aged five, in Max Reinhardt's *Midsummer Night's Dream* (1935) and the visual richness of that production deeply affected him. His pre-1947 (teenage) films emphasize the enjoyment of dressing-up and the ritual it involves. *The Nest* (1943)—a story of incest disturbed leading to violence—contains a scene of 'absolutions, the acts of dressing- and making-up, observed as a magic rite'. *Tinsel Tree* (1941–2) is an even more elemental statement. A Christmas tree is (ritually) dressed up in sparkling decorations (perhaps influenced by Reinhardt's wood), then stripped bare and burnt in a burst of hand-tinting.

Fireworks (1947; plate 41), his first work as a 'public' film-maker, is unique in Anger's *œuvre* in its complete rejection of Hollywood. If any nostalgia exists, it is in the imagery—the broken plaster hand, the burning photographs of the dream—which recalls the poetic artifice of Cocteau in *Le Sang d'un Poète*. Anger corresponded with Cocteau (as did Markopoulos) and worked with him briefly on several abortive projects during the early fifties, but he did not share Cocteau's literary style. Anger required a more potent form. In *Puce Moment* (1949), a fragment of a larger work, and in *La Lune des Lapins* (1950), he returned to Hollywood material, the first being 'the ritual of dressing and going out' of a twenties' movie star; the second, another resurrection of Reinhardt's tinselled wood—this time as a setting for a Pierrot (who causes chaos with his magic lantern!).

With *Eaux d'Artifice* (1953), Anger quietly made a masterpiece—a complete fusion of idea and technique. A woman (a circus dwarf in baroque wig and costume) hurries between the moonlit fountains of the Tivoli Gardens in Rome, seeking who knows what? The film is printed on a cold, uniformly blue stock; the images, often in slow motion—freezing the water yet letting it move (more explicitly)—dissolve one through to another, defying any attempts to determine the point of transition. Grotesque faces (carved water-spirits), shadows, piles of water and the fluttering image of the woman move into the screen in succession, the climax being a purely visual one, so underplayed as to be scarcely visible—the woman spreads her fan and it flickers, hand-tinted, green. Then she 'melts'—becomes a fountain—the water momentarily takes her shape as she disappears. In *The Inauguration of the Pleasure Dome* (1954, re-edited 1966; plate 42), and in his subsequent films, Anger introduces a conscious element of alchemy, which gives the eclectic range of his subjects a new significance. His nostalgia for Hollywood, his almost academic montage (*Scorpio Rising*) and his combination of 'pop' and mythology are given a new potency as the tools of his magic. In *Pleasure Dome* ('an invocation of Horus, the crowned and conquering child, the godhead of the aquarian age'), one is aware of the magic ritual only on a secondary level, subservient to both the multi-layered images and Janacek's amazing music (*The Glagolitic Mass*); some strange purpose seems to order the movements of the participants, but that is all.

In *Scorpio Rising* (1963), Anger's ' "high" view of the myth of the American motorcyclist', the ritual is more explicit—the worship of the bike, the dressing of the Angels, the orgy and the ultimate self-destruction. Parallels are drawn with the magic of Christianity (clips from *King of Kings*), Dean, Brando, comic strips, and above all pop-music (the revelation of the homo-erotic substructure of '*Fools Rush in . . .*', '*Blue Velvet . . .*', '*Wind me up . . .*', etc., must surely make them immortal). Curiously, the film taken overall is almost puritanically moral—the crudest message being the double one ' "speed" kills' (as in *Heatwave* leading to *Wipeout*). The magic exists only on an incidental level—each act is celebrated (filmed with the utmost sympathy)—so why the moral tone of the final destruction?

In *KKK* (*Kustom Kar Kommandos*) (1964; plate 43), Anger gives his purest observation of ritual taken to the point of fetishism—the creative act (the building of the dream buggy) is over—the builder polishes it with a vast, useless powder-puff. *Invocation of My Demon Brother* (1969), a rescued and reworked section of the stolen *Lucifer Rising* (1966–7), is Anger's most recent and most consistently inventive work. Its style is a departure from the classic 'Russian' editing of *Scorpio* and would seem to indicate the beginning of a more informal, but no less energetic and well structured approach to his subject. The power of this movie is conveyed by movement within the image: by the rapid flickering of the eyeballs of the albino male and by the figure of Anger himself, seen always in speeded-up long shots and jagged zooms—spinning and casting all his energy into the void that surrounds him. The re-made *Lucifer Rising* which he announced in 1970 threatens to be a powerful movie.

The camera assistant on Harrington's *Fragment of Seeking* was Gregory J. Markopoulos, a student of Von Sternberg's at the University of Southern California, now one of the most respected film-makers of the New American Cinema.

Markopoulos' highly personal style is the product of a consistent evolution that began with the trilogy *Du Sang de la Volupté et de la Mort* (1948). Then, as now, he was concerned with the re-activation of the narrative film form, but nothing could be more foreign to his work than the accepted language of close-, mid-, long-shots, 'follow-the-action' camera movements and nondescript editing that typify the commercial film story. In the three parts of the trilogy (*Psyche*, *Lysis* and *Charmides*) he establishes at once his rejection of 'normal' continuity, replacing it with a fragmented approach in which the sum of the images is almost more important than their sequence. In *Lysis* (the description is Sitney's):

> An ugly woman pops from one tree to another by means of stop motion photography; a young man, lying in bed, rubs his feet along decoration streams; Markopoulos wanders through a graveyard; a nude man, hanging by his wrists, is stabbed in the back; a negress plays with a swan. The spectator soon becomes lost in a maze of strange images. Like the protagonist, we are hypnotized by what we see . . .

The theme of the trilogy is homosexual love (male and female); he tempers it, as often in his work, with free but appropriate interpretations of classical literature and mythology.

As an extension of the subject fragmentation, Markopoulos has developed an editing technique entirely his own, using short bursts (groups) of images—single frames taken from different scenes or parts of a scene, both repeating and anticipating events. These 'thought images', which arrived in their mature form in *Twice a Man* (1963), serve both as a mental–emotional counterpoint to the longer 'base' shots (paraphrasing the multiplicity of consciousness of the central character, or simply keeping the viewer aware of the physical complexity of the event) and as an important kinetic contribution, allowing the 'base' shots to become more formal and static in contrast.

In *Psyche*, this development is hinted at in the rapid recapitulation of the major scenes in the final minutes. In *Lysis*, the shots Sitney describes are all static (no camera movement) and equal in length—the editing being performed entirely in-camera. The film is projected as shot. Markopoulos developed this discipline in later works, in *Ming Green* (1966), *Through a Lens Brightly: Mark Turbyfill* (1966) and in the portraits, *Galaxie* (1966) and *Political Portraits* (1969), taking it to unprecedented heights. The rewind mechanism and frame counter of the Bolex camera, which he uses almost exclusively, allow him to make superimpositions, frame clusters and complete rearrangements of the time-scale in sequences while photographing them, adding a new dimension to the process. With the growth of the 'underground' movement, the use of in-camera techniques has become quite widespread, but Markopoulos' formal application has remained unique. No other film-maker save Brakhage can make as complete statements from so little material. In *Ming Green* Markopoulos creates, through a series of overlapping and interrupted images, a still-life of a flat in New York (his own), objects, still photographs, colours, etc., linked and contrasted by 'thought images'. In *Himself as Herself* (1966) the repressed (male/female) duality of the central character is suggested in a 'human still-life' lasting nearly an hour. In a later work, *Gammelion* (1967), a 'fable' in the form of an exploration of Il Castello Roccasinibalda, the entire film is created in short image clusters introduced and ended by black-to-white fades.

Markopoulos' use of sound is no less sophisticated. Again, *Twice a Man* revealed the mature style. The original script included brief exchanges of dialogue that related, but were not synchronized, to the action; in a second preparation they were reduced to key words and phrases, to be spoken 'without translation into meaning', that is 'spoken as they would be in daily life', and in this version he recorded it. For the first time ever, a film-maker makes the assumption that if images can be chopped up and given significance in a non-ordinary sequence (the basic premise of the edited film), then so perhaps can words. The device is extraordinarily successful, and Markopoulos repeats it in his interpretation of Aeschylus' play *Prometheus Bound—The Illiac Passion* (1964–6). In *Twice a Man* the word clusters are accompanied by blocks of sound, which act as their 'basic image'. Thus the film begins with a four-minute block of rain pattering, introduced by a clap of thunder, while the screen remains in darkness. Markopoulos established at once the importance of sound, which works hereafter in counterpoint to the other elements.

Since *Gammelion*, Markopoulos has been working in Europe and has largely withdrawn from the American scene. His European works have included two operas for Bavarian television, the longer one *Alter Action* being edited directly on Ampex videotape equipment, using his distinctive technique, and a feature *Mysteries* (1968) shot in Munich.

Like Anger and Markopoulos, Stan Brakhage also established a reputation as a film-artist even before the co-operative movement began. Of the three, Brakhage's contribution has been by far the most radical—the subject matter and techniques of his works are completely foreign to the (once) accepted concepts of the serious film. His films have no story, no symbolism, no acting, no posed photographic beauty; the drama is the drama of the skies, light and shadow, movement, trees, windows, people, corners, animals, single blades of grass—in fact, the drama of vision, a vision that implies a belief that the first priority is to see and record, the second to structure and interpret. Editing, in Brakhage's work, is not the construction of a cause and effect sequence but a recontexting of images with the intention of re-examining their meaning and relationship.

Ernest Callenbach, editor of *Film Quarterly*, ended a short review of five of Brakhage's earliest mature works (five subsequent to *Anticipation of the Night*) with:

> This particular lack of intensity, of artistry, is not a matter of ideas or of dramatic sense in the ordinary connotation of the term. It is the absence of a rare quality which critics refer to, mystically perhaps, by saying such-and-such a film-maker has an 'eye'—film-makers like Bergman or Ray, who both (though in almost diametrically opposite realms) have the gift of creating a debonair surface beneath which some kind of structural or associative logic binds like iron.[1]

Earlier, Callenbach talks about Brakhage's '. . . odd filters or exposure . . . odd shapes, some recognizable, some not, cats, nude

[1] *Film Quarterly*, Spring 1961.

bodies glimpsed, cut very rapidly, but without grace, without what would correspond in film to "musical ideas".'

To look at Brakhage's films hoping to find surface beauty and the obvious correlation of the image-flow to known musical forms (a basic ingredient of most 'accompanied' films from Fischinger to the Hollywood feature) is to look for something completely opposed to what they offer. The rhythm of his films is the rhythm of the camera, twenty-four frames per second, or more, or less; the eye—increased blink-rate in time of crisis—rapid change of focus; the memory—the rate at which image-recall operates; and the body—breathing, heartbeat, childbirth contractions, etc. Their beauty is the beauty of the object revealed.

Brakhage now lives and works with his family in the mountains of Colorado. He spent most of his childhood in Denver, and it was there that he made his first film, *Interim*, in 1953.

His movie education was largely in San Francisco, partly at the Institute of Fine Arts (where Peterson gave him the anamorphic lens he had used on *Lead Shoes*) and partly through the companionship of San Francisco's community of artists and poets. On trips back to Denver he set up the Denver Theater in a war-surplus tent, performing Wedekind, Strindberg and Chekhov, and shooting *Unglassed Windows cast a Terrible Reflection* (1953) and *Desistfilm* (1954). In *Desistfilm*, about a drunken teenage party, he already demonstrates his extraordinary control of rapid camera movement.

Then, with *In Between*, a portrait of Jess Collins set to music by John Cage, *The Way to the Shadow Garden* and *Reflections on Black* (all 1955), he entered a period of 'nightmare' psychodramas, the second two using lack of vision, blindness, as their central metaphor. *Reflections* was made in New York where Brakhage became involved with the Gryphon Group and established a friendship with Maya Deren. *The Wonder Ring* (1955), another film made there, at the suggestion of Joseph Cornell, suddenly revealed an (intuitive) visual emphasis in his work. A record of the now-demolished Third Avenue elevated railway, Brakhage, making his first use of colour, concentrates his camera on the semi-abstract multiple window reflections and natural montage created by the train's movement through the landscape.

He made one more 'pure' psychodrama, *Flesh of Morning* (1956), a subjective study of masturbation, before confirming his change of direction in *Nightcats* (1956)—an abstraction of shapes of cats moving in a pool of light.

These apparently divergent interests were to fuse in *Anticipation of the Night* (1958), in which a complex flow of images (representing the lyrical, visual links between events seen through the uncomplicated eyes of childhood) is interrupted by the shadow figure of the artist who, unequal to the child's vision, commits suicide at the end. The apparent lack of formal structure in *Anticipation* provoked severe criticism from Brakhage's increasing number of admirers, but it has since become recognized as a key work in his development, being the first to show his growing confidence in the intuitive (as opposed to the predetermined) interpretation of image and human drama.

In *Metaphors on Vision*—a collection of his written works put together by P. Adams Sitney for *Film Culture* in 1963—Brakhage records his awareness at this time of the developing relationship between the treatment of his subjects and his own subconscious conflicts. *Loving* (1956) successfully projected his concept of an ideal male/female relationship (as personified by his friends James Tenney and Carolee Schneemann; the impracticality of trying to relate his own recent marriage to theirs was only made apparent to him through the process of filming *Cat's Cradle* (1959)—his record of some time the couples spent together.

This recognition of the interchange between 'art' and 'life' was almost ritualized in *Wedlock House: An Intercourse* (1959), another film made immediately after his marriage, in which Brakhage and his wife Jane re-created an argument in an attempt both to understand it and to rediscover each other. The main body of the film is structured by the passing back and forth between them of the camera and a portable light; which was intended to give balance to the argument—it works beautifully as a formal aesthetic device.

As his confidence increased, Brakhage took on increasingly more abstract subjects: in *Sirius Remembered* (1959), the ambiguity of emotions aroused by the decomposing body of a much-loved family dog, expressed through wild, lyrical camera movements about its corpse; in *Mothlight* (1963), a literal re-creation of moth movement and vision made by sealing moths' wings, flowers, blades of grass between strips of clear film (plate 36); in *Pasht* (1965), an incredibly tightly-edited play of light (on the coat of a cat in the process of giving birth).

As Brakhage's family grew, so it became included in his films, his loving studies of childbirth, childhood and family life—*Window Water Baby Moving* (1959), *Thigh Line Lyre Triangular* (1961), *Films by Stan Brakhage* (1961), *Three Films* (1965)—are possibly his most widely appreciated works.

But all these works are as preparatory studies for his two great undertakings of the sixties—*Dog Star Man/The Art of Vision* (1961–5) and the *Songs* (1964 onwards). The seventy minutes of

Dog Star Man are divided into a prelude and four sections; Michael McClure gives an account of the thematic material:

> In *Dog Star Man*, all possible views are taken, the Man dressed in ragged pants and boots with beard and hair to his shoulders, accompanied by his dog, struggles up the mountainside fleeing *to* a holocaust that may be real or imaginary—but the man is real! We see man and dog . . . the hand fights in the snow for a new grip upon icy rock . . . then a passage of whiteness with an almost invisible pattern of pink within it . . . cloud . . . mountain . . . canyon . . . dog . . . tree . . . blackness . . . solar corona . . . internal organ . . . bloodstream . . . blackness . . . part of face brooding against sky . . . the man falls . . . the season changes . . . he climbs . . . the memory, or fantasy, of the man dancing naked to the waist like a messiah in flickering firelight . . . he faints, struggles and hallucinates, becoming immortal in his striving . . . The camera is outside the man photographing him . . . the camera is an eye inside of the man seeing his organs . . . The camera does not distinguish between future fantasy and past memory of the man . . . The camera does not say whether it is inside of the man's organs or the dog's organs. The camera does not say when the outer world is imagined or when it is real.

These same images, original footage, stock footage, hand-painting (Brakhage's 'closed-eye-vision'—nothing could be less like the compositions of Lye and McLaren), scratches and actual film collages (one image physically inserted into another) are given epic proportions in the four-and-a-half-hour *Art of Vision*, in which Brakhage extends the visual themes of the earlier work (by running the A, B, C and D rolls separately) into a symphonic structure.

The *Songs* are works on 8 mm, a change prompted partly by his concern to make films available for purchase and home use at low cost (an ambition shared by Bruce Conner) and partly by the intrinsic challenge of the smaller gauge. The shorter *Songs* are mostly hymns to daily life and represent the very essence of subjective camera work—the interplay of mental and optical imagery. In *Song 23*, the *23rd Psalm Branch*, he again used stock footage—second world war newsreels—to make an 'investigation of the image of war itself', almost a kinetic study of the patterns of war and how they relate to the domestic environment, a subject provoked by television coverage of the Vietnam war.

Most of Brakhage's films since *Anticipation of the Night* have been silent, the exceptions being *Blue Moses*, an untypical piece about the role of the actor, and the beautiful *Fire of Waters* (1965) in which sounds abstracted from a dog's bark and a woman in childbirth share the film with a nocturnal rooftop landscape that is revealed by intermittent flashes of lightning. The first section of the new series *Scenes from Under Childhood* (1968 onwards) was completed with sound but Brakhage has since announced that he considered this to have been an aesthetic mistake, as it detracts from the 'instant by instant' manifestation of the visual, and he intends, therefore, to avoid its use in the future.

1 The essential structure of the narrative film: a frame from each sequence of Edwin S. Porter's *The Life of an American Fireman* 1902–3.

2 Drawings by Emile Cohl (1909): Cohl shared his contemporary Méliès' delight in phantasmagoria, a concept that survived in 'commercial' cinema only in the special effects department but which continued to provide animators as diverse as Dave Fleischer, Norman McLaren, Douglas Crockwell and Stan Vanderbeek with the mainspring of their art.

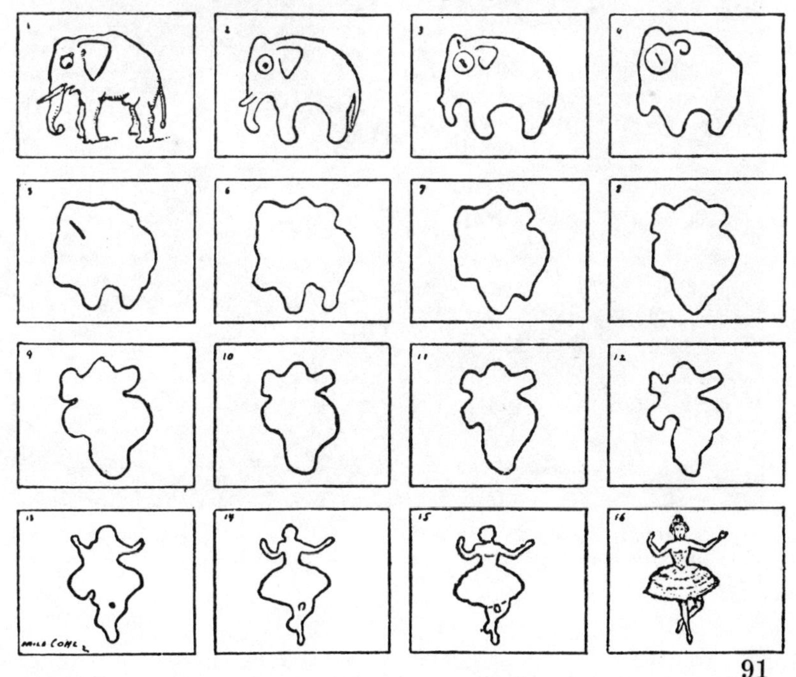

3 The collaboration of graphic artists in the French avant-garde: sets by Fernand Léger and Alberto Cavalcanti in Marcel L'Herbier's *L'Inhumaine* 1923.

4 Classical Russian cutting as evolved independently in France by Dimitri Kirsanov in *Ménilmontant* 1924: the axe murder (left); the young girl discovers the bodies of her parents (right).

5 Abel Gance, the innovator, was the one French 'commercial' film-maker to receive the praise of the Paris avant-garde. *La Folie du Docteur Tube* 1915 shows his use of distorting lenses which predates the German vogue for similar effects (for instance, as in Metzner's *Uberfall*).

6 Gance's use of rapid cutting in *La Roue* 1923. Much admired by the Russians, this technique in its more schematic form became 'Russian cutting' or 'montage'.

7 Photographed abstractions from Man Ray's *Emak Bakia* 1926.

8 Man Ray's use of multi-screen in *L'Etoile de Mer* 1928, a technique introduced by Gance in his *Napoléon* 1926.

9 Film becomes the subject of film: part of the loop of a woman climbing stairs in Fernand Léger's *Ballet Mécanique* 1924.

10 The visual pun: a rotorelief from Marcel Duchamp's *Anemic Cinema* 1926.

9

10

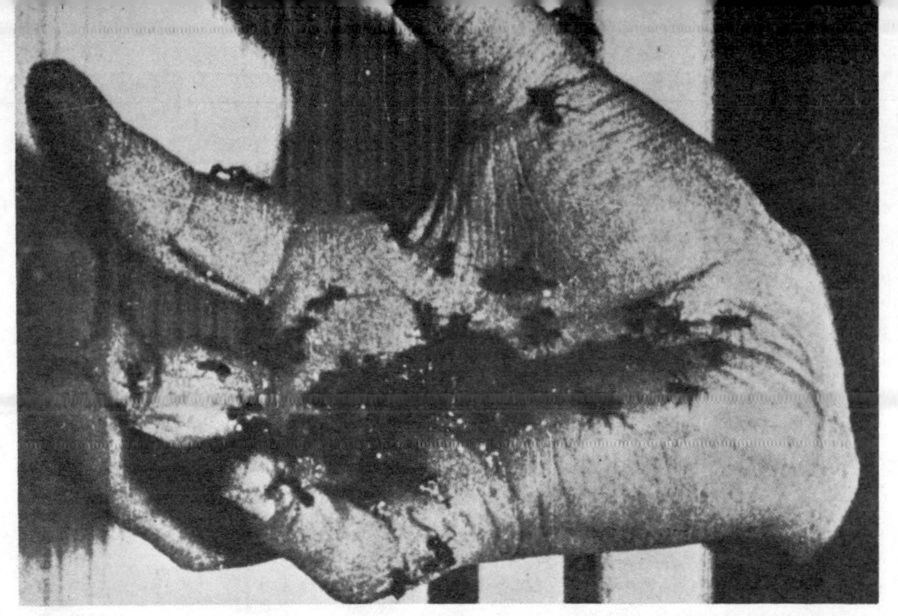

11 Salvador Dali's and Luis Buñuel's celebrated *Un Chien Andalou* 1927.

12 and 13 Jean Cocteau with his muse (above) and as she appears in *Le Sang d'un Poète* 1930 (opposite).

14 The first 'absolute' film:
Viking Eggeling's *Diagonal Symphony* 1920–2.

15 Hans Richter's *Film Study* 1926.

16 to 20 Walter Ruttman's *Berlin, the Symphony of a Great City* 1927: the 'city symphony', created almost simultaneously in Russia, France and Germany, became the first immediately accessible (popular) avant-garde art form.

21 and 22 Ruttman's *Berlin, the Symphony of a Great City* 1927.

Frei

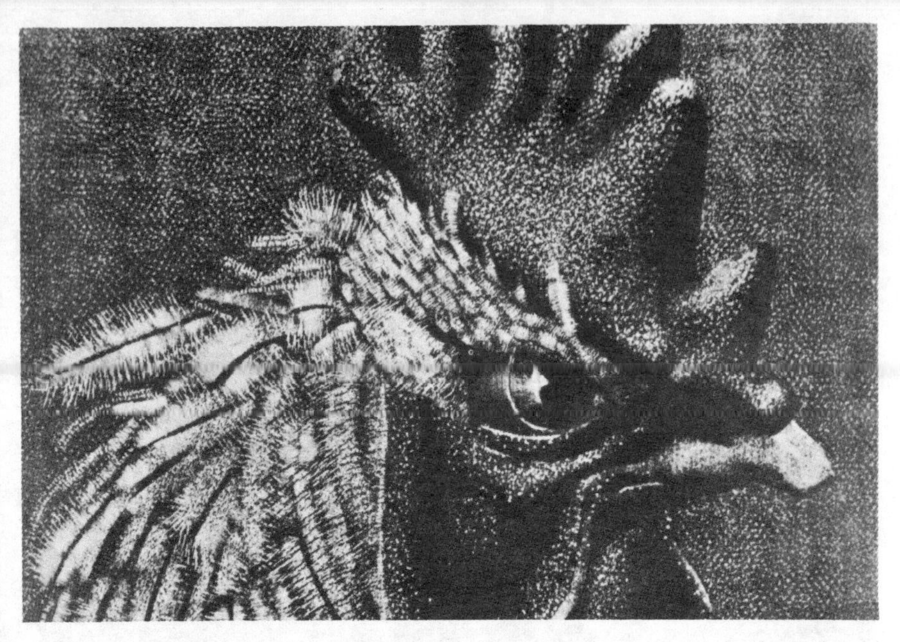

23 One and a half million pins, moved frame by frame, created Alexandre Alexeieff's and Clair Parker's *En Passant* 1943.

24 Lye's *Rainbow Dance* 1936: the kinetic use of colour separations in the optical printer.

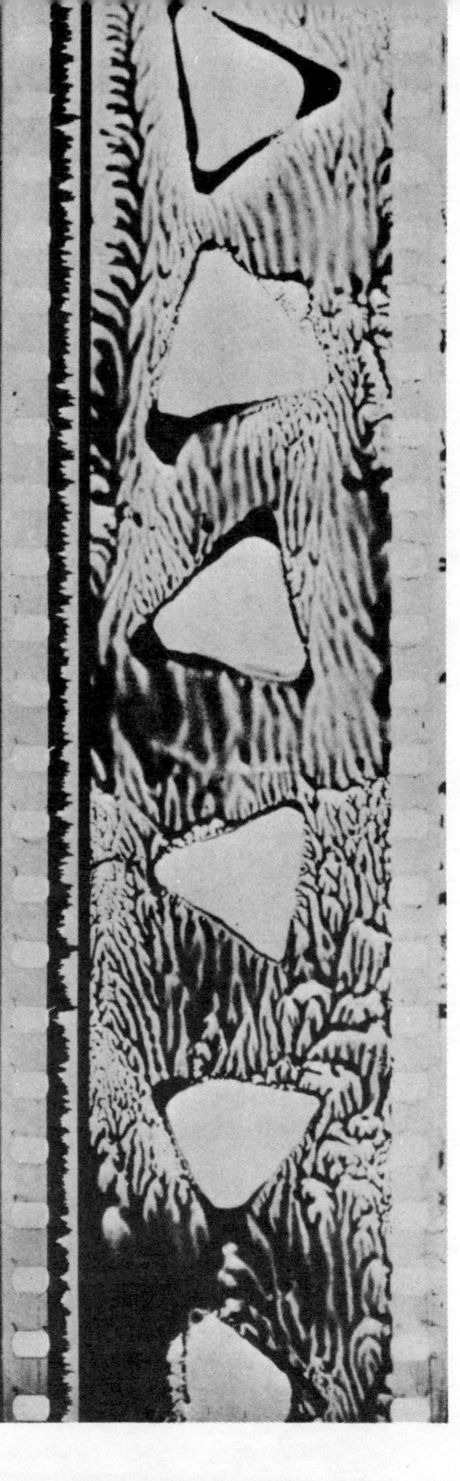

25 Len Lye's *Colour Box* 1935: the first film shown publicly in which the images were hand-painted directly on to the emulsion.

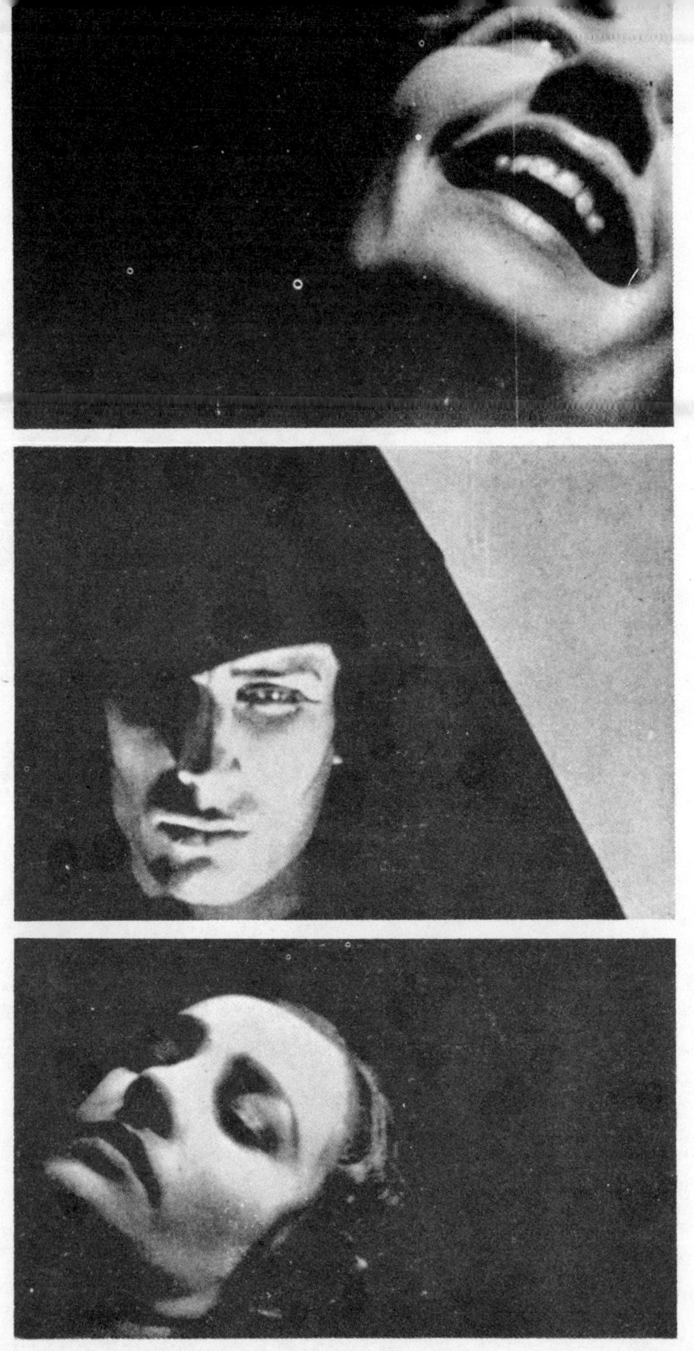

26 The American avant-garde:
Watson and Webber's *Lot in Sodom* 1933.

27 An early glass shot (1908) by special effects pioneer Norman O. Dawn. Dawn painted on glass, placed between the camera and the scene to be photographed, to re-create the roof of a derelict building in Tasmania.

28 Dawn's *A Girl in the Dark* 1917: a painted matte transforms Griffith Park, Los Angeles, into a Tibetan landscape.

29 'A hundred and one ways to wipe': a number of the trick transitions created by Lynn Dunn for the Ginger Rogers and Fred Astaire picture *Flying Down to Rio* 1933.

30 Special effects by Fred Sersen in Clarence Brown's *The Rains Came* 1938: extras and miniature models combined by using mattes (hand-painted travelling mattes were used to create the effect of masonry falling in front of the extras—not shown here).

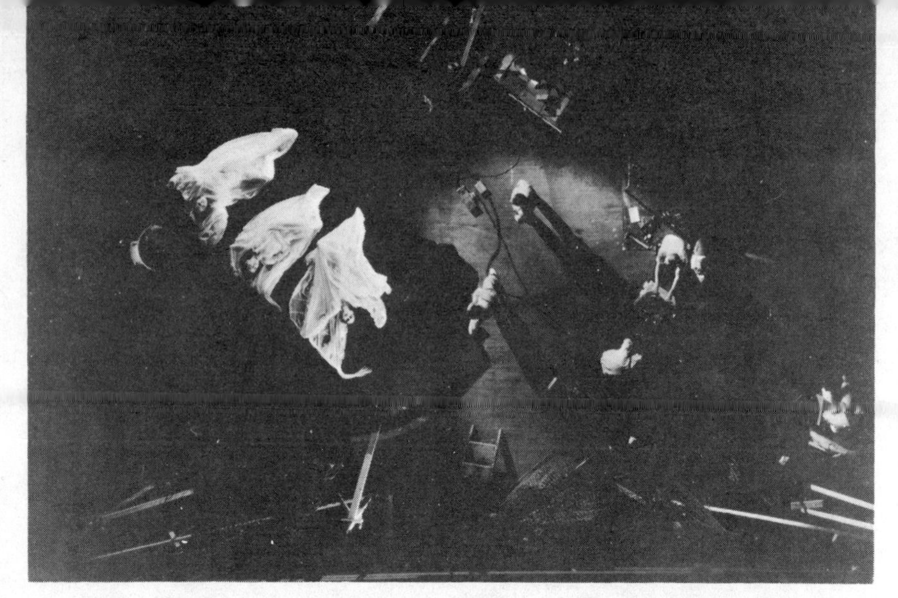

31 An aerial view of the stage floor on which montage artist Slavko Vorkapich created the rise and flight of the Furies in *Crime without Passion* 1934.

32 Marie Menken, an amateur in the most beautiful sense of the word, with her camera.

33 Oskar Fischinger's *Composition in Blue* 1933: the success of this film brought Fischinger to Hollywood where he provided the first link between West Coast abstract film-makers and the European avant-garde.

34 Fischinger working on *Motion Painting No 1* 1949.

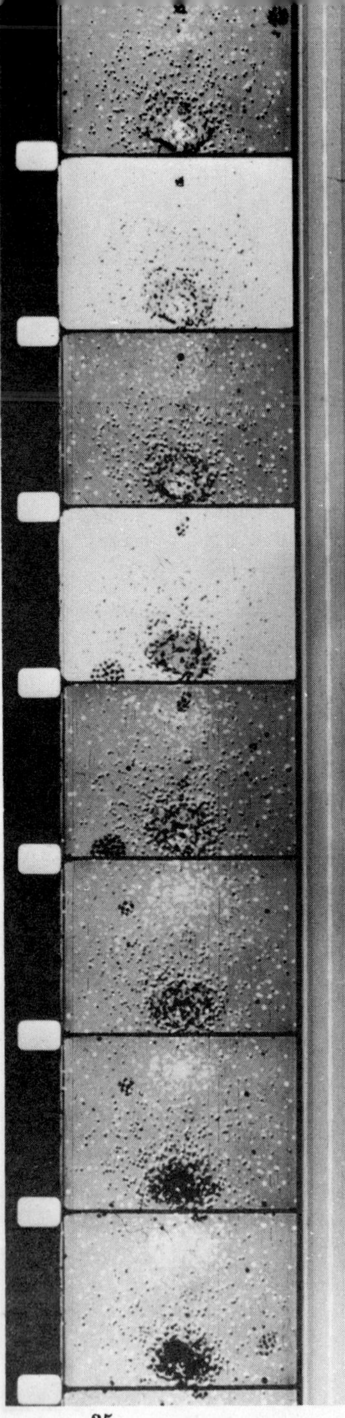

35

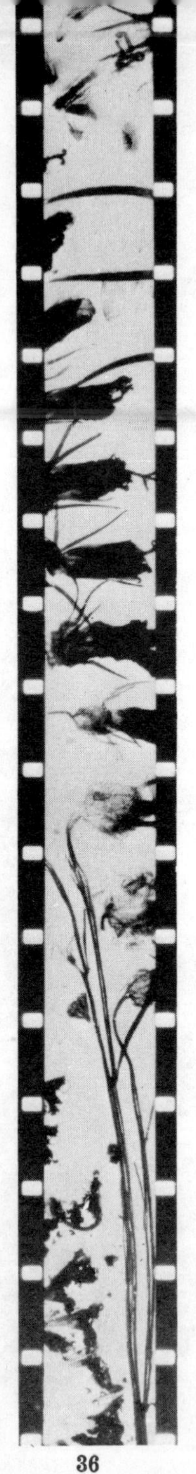

36

35 James Whitney's *Yantra* 1950–7: alternate frame flicker and computer-like complexity in a film a generation ahead of its time.

36 Stan Brakhage's *Mothlight* 1963: moth's wings, flower petals and blades of grass held between two clear strips of film create a flickering image that Brakhage describes as 'what a moth would see from birth to death if black were white and white were black'.

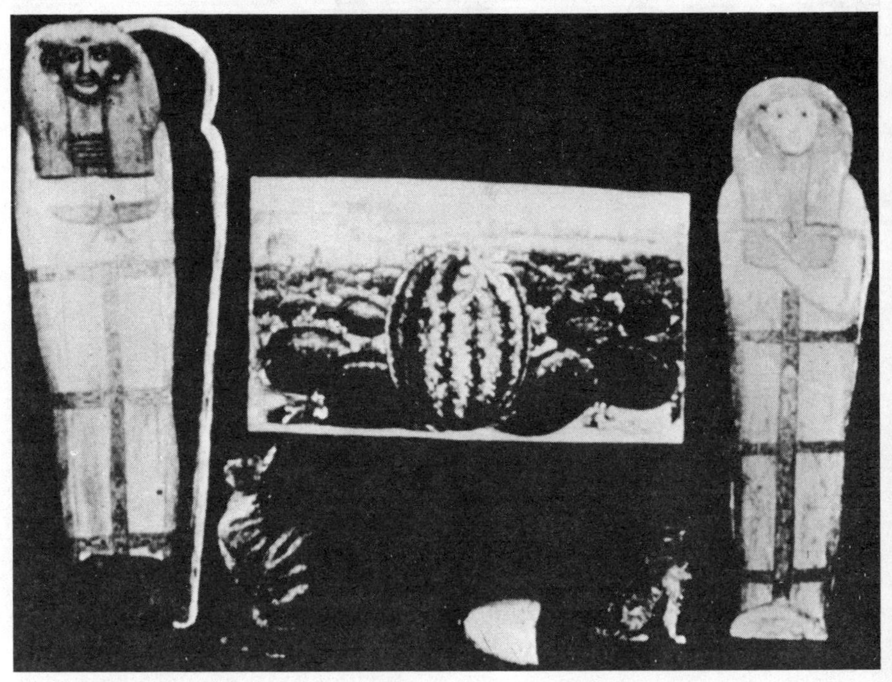

37 Harry Smith's *Heaven and Earth Magic* 1957–62: an extension of the surrealist principle of automatism into the world of the animated collage—'all the permutations possible were built up'.

38 James Broughton, the film poet, in his own film *The Adventures of Jimmy* 1950.

39 Introspective cinema: Curtis Harrington's *On the Edge* 1949.

40 Harrington's *Fragment of Seeking* 1946.

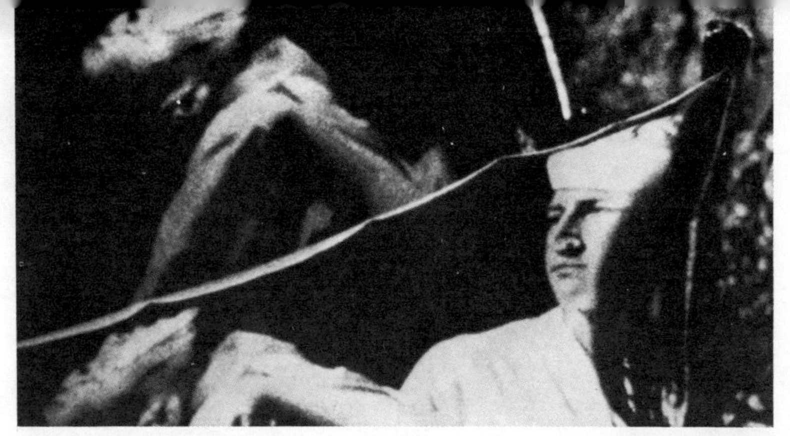

41 The independent cinema's coming of age: Kenneth Anger's *Fireworks* 1947, showing the burning image of the film-maker and his sailor/lover.

42 Anger's *The Inauguration of the Pleasure Dome* 1954: Anger complements the technical perfection of his images with almost subliminal editing.

43 Anger's *KKK* (*Kustom Kar Kommandos*) 1964: 'The All-Chrome Ruby Plush Dream Buggy and its Maker.'

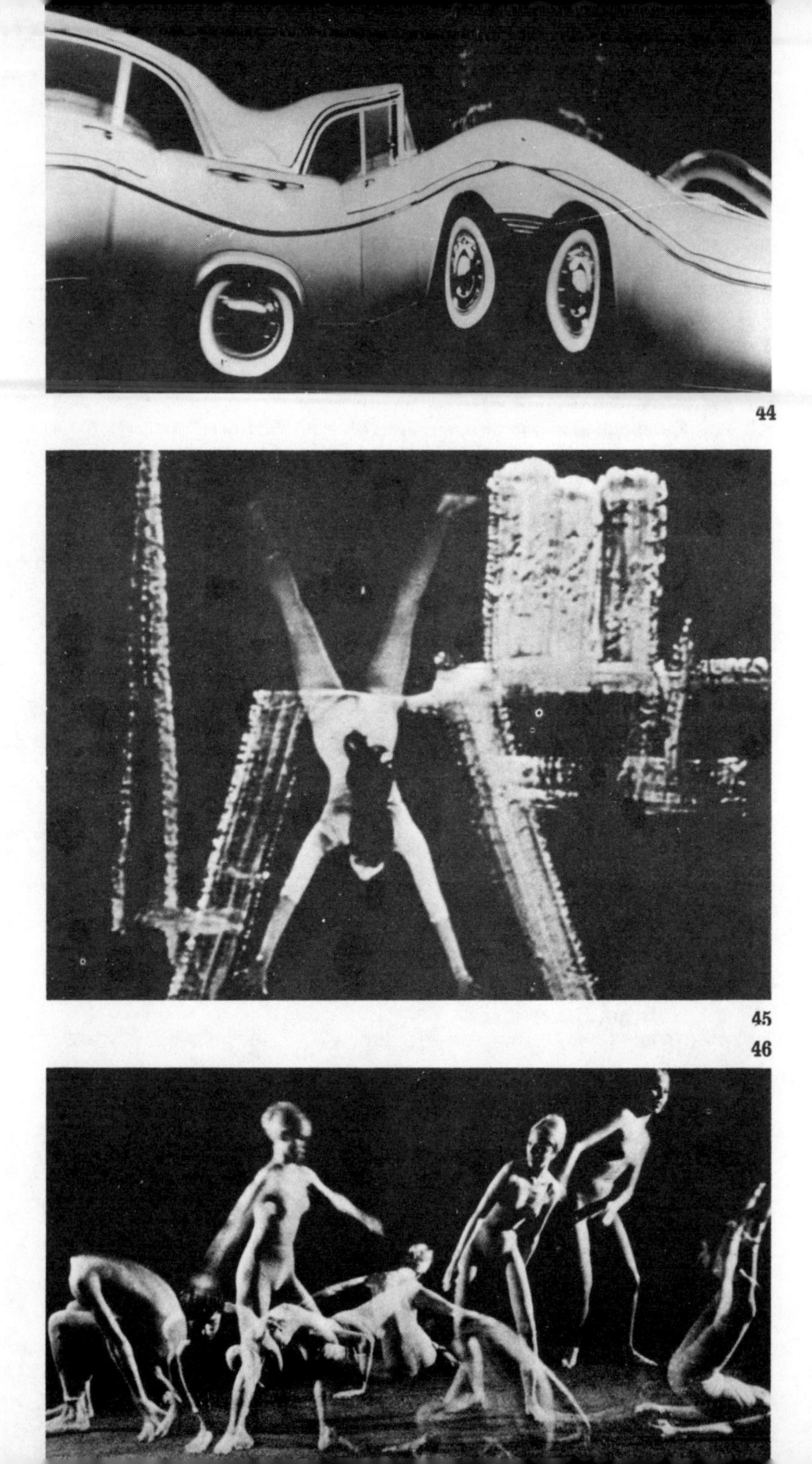

44

45

46

47 Shirley Clarke's *Bridges go Round* 1958.

44 Francis Thomson's *NY, NY* 1957: artistry through distortion.

45 Ed Emshwiller's *Dance Chromatic* 1959.

46 Emshwiller's *Image Flesh and Voice* 1969.

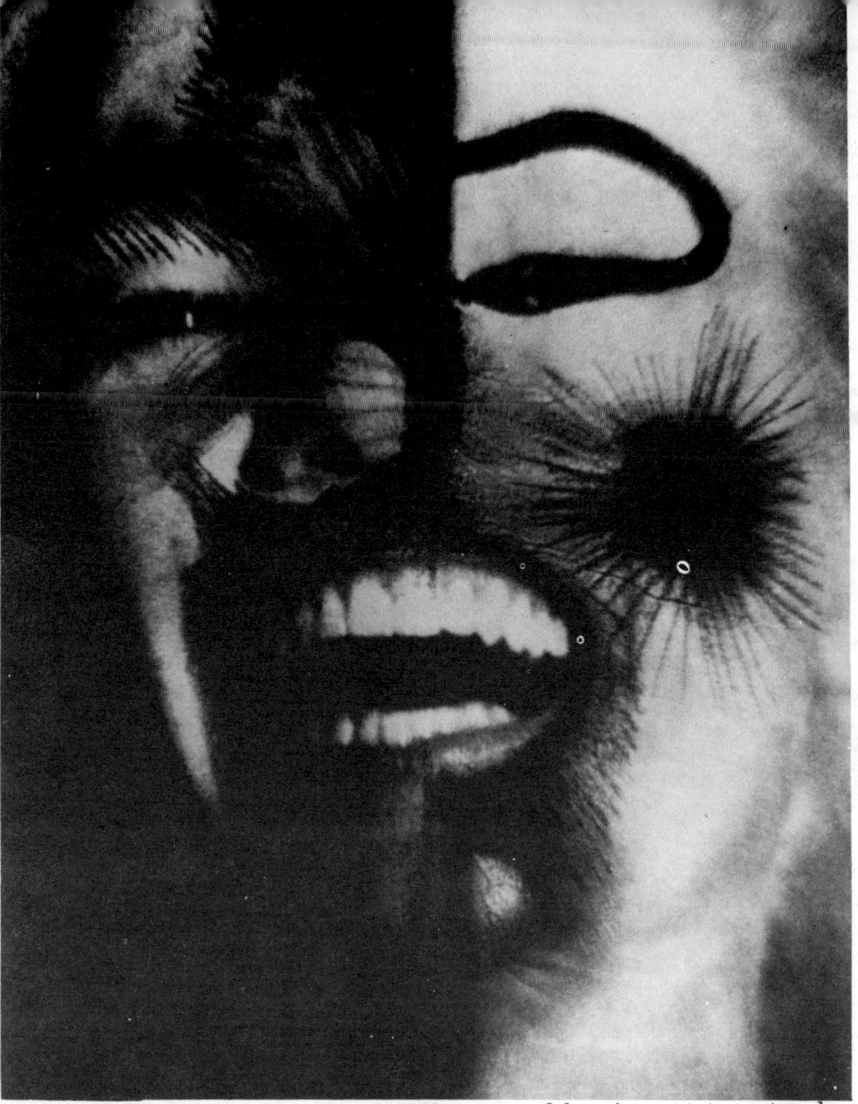

48 Stan Vanderbeek's *Breathdeath* 1963: a powerful anti-war statement and one of the most accomplished collage animations.

49 *Poemfield* 1968 Vanderbeek and Ken Knowlton: 'the range in tones created by programming the surface of a television tube to be filled with the different letters and characters of a typewriter keyboard', resulting in one of the most successful animations of computer graphics.

50 and 51 Bruce Baillie's *Castro Street* 1966: 'inspired by a lesson from Erik Satie; a film in the form of a street'. Combining 'all visual and sound elements from the street', Baillie creates in-camera travelling mattes by masking the lens with a black-gloved hand (below).

49

50, 51

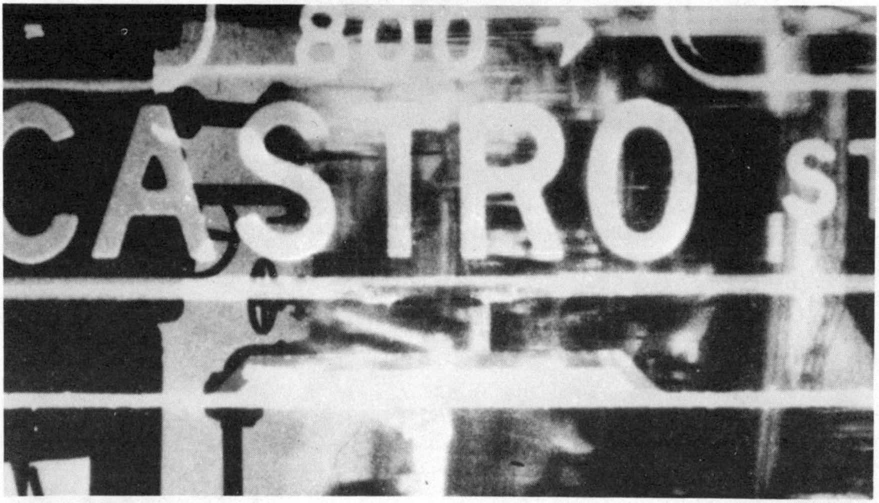

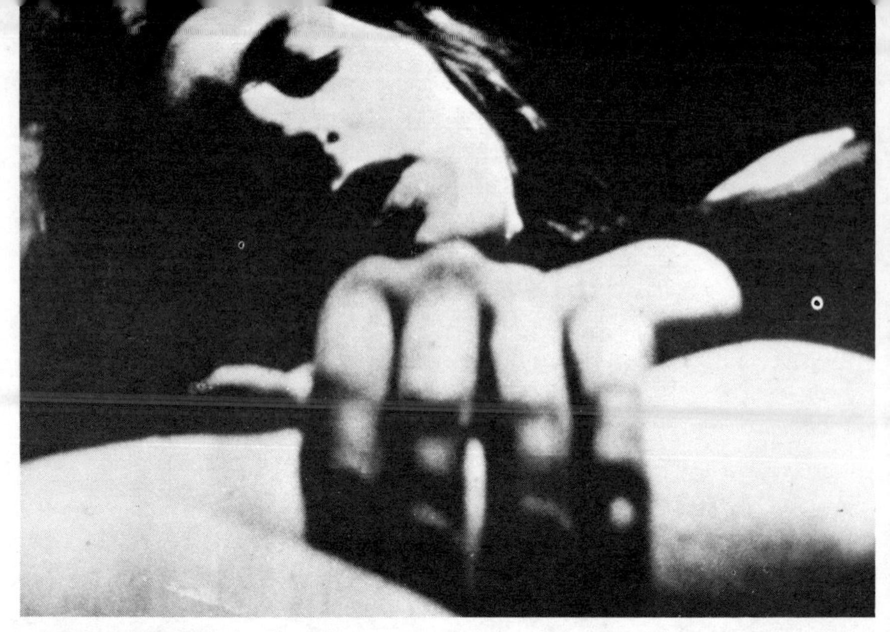

52 Steve Dwoskin's *Alone* 1964.

53 O'Neill's *Coming Down*: phased printing of rock musicians yields triplicate images, each a different colour, one a few seconds behind the other in motion; meanwhile a superimposed neon Buddha slaps his knees with delight.

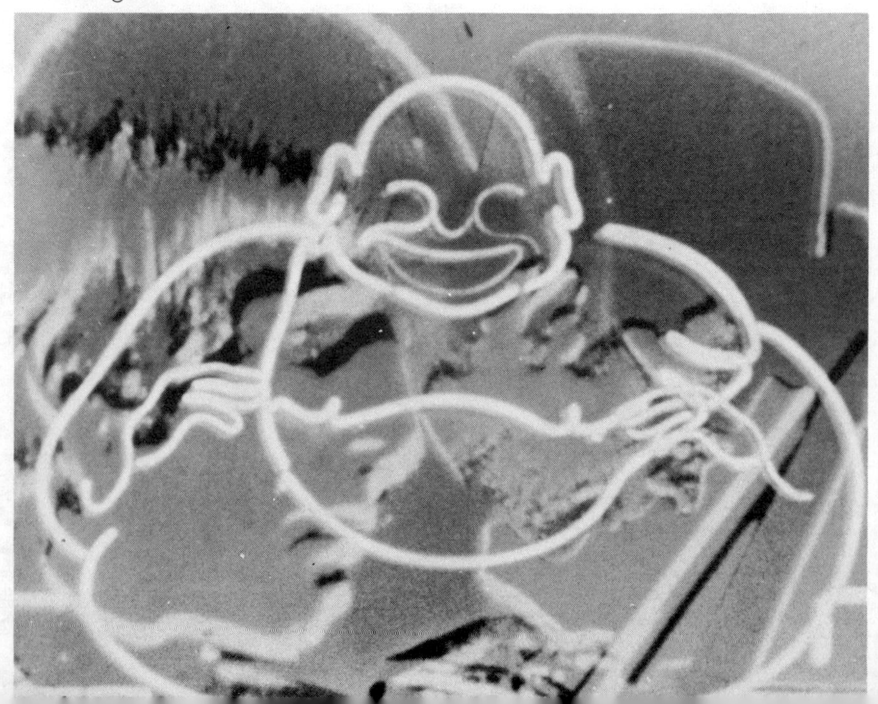

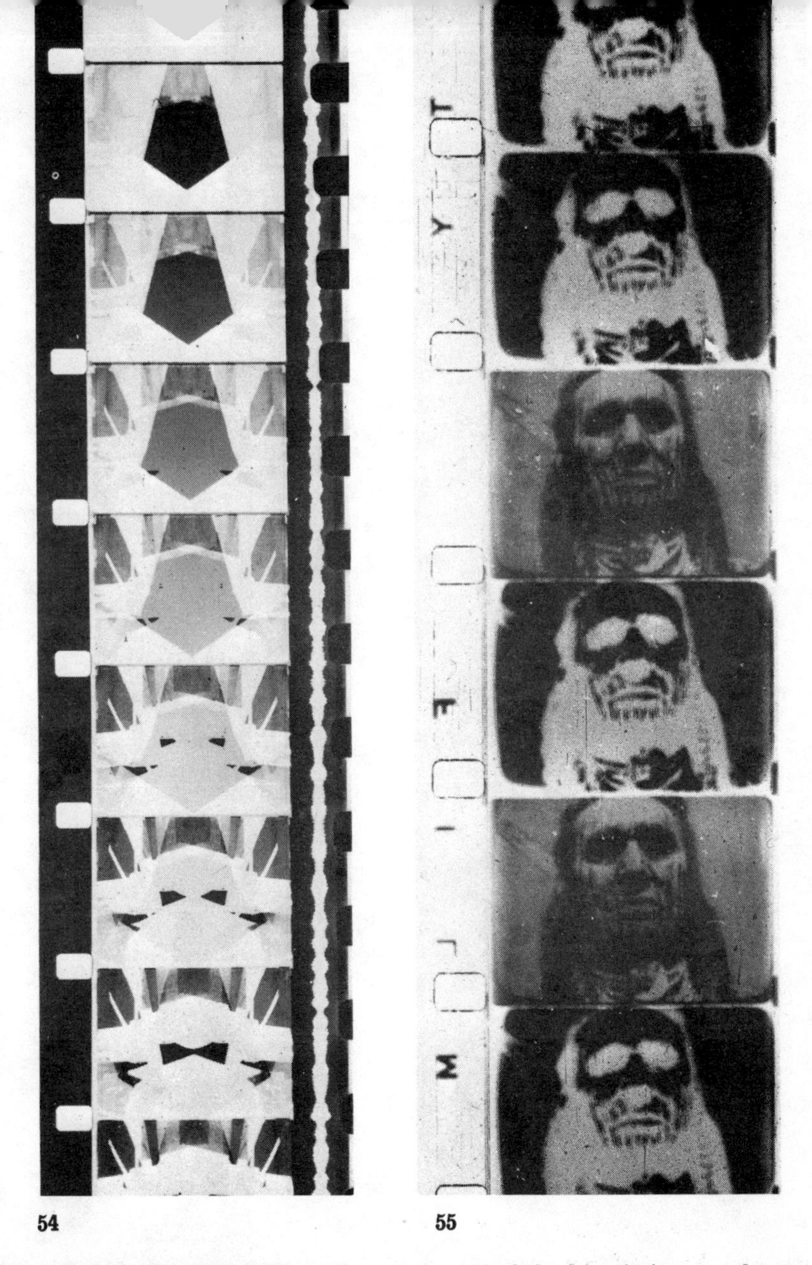

54 Pat O'Neill's *7362* 1965–7: the supremacy of the kinetic image—shapes extracted from an oil pump change colour and cross-fade into shapes abstracted and duplicated (mirrorwise) from a dancing girl.

55 Burton Gershfield's *Now that the Buffalo's Gone* 1967: solarized colour and alternate frame flicker evoke the white man's aggression, in a hymn to the vanishing Red Indian.

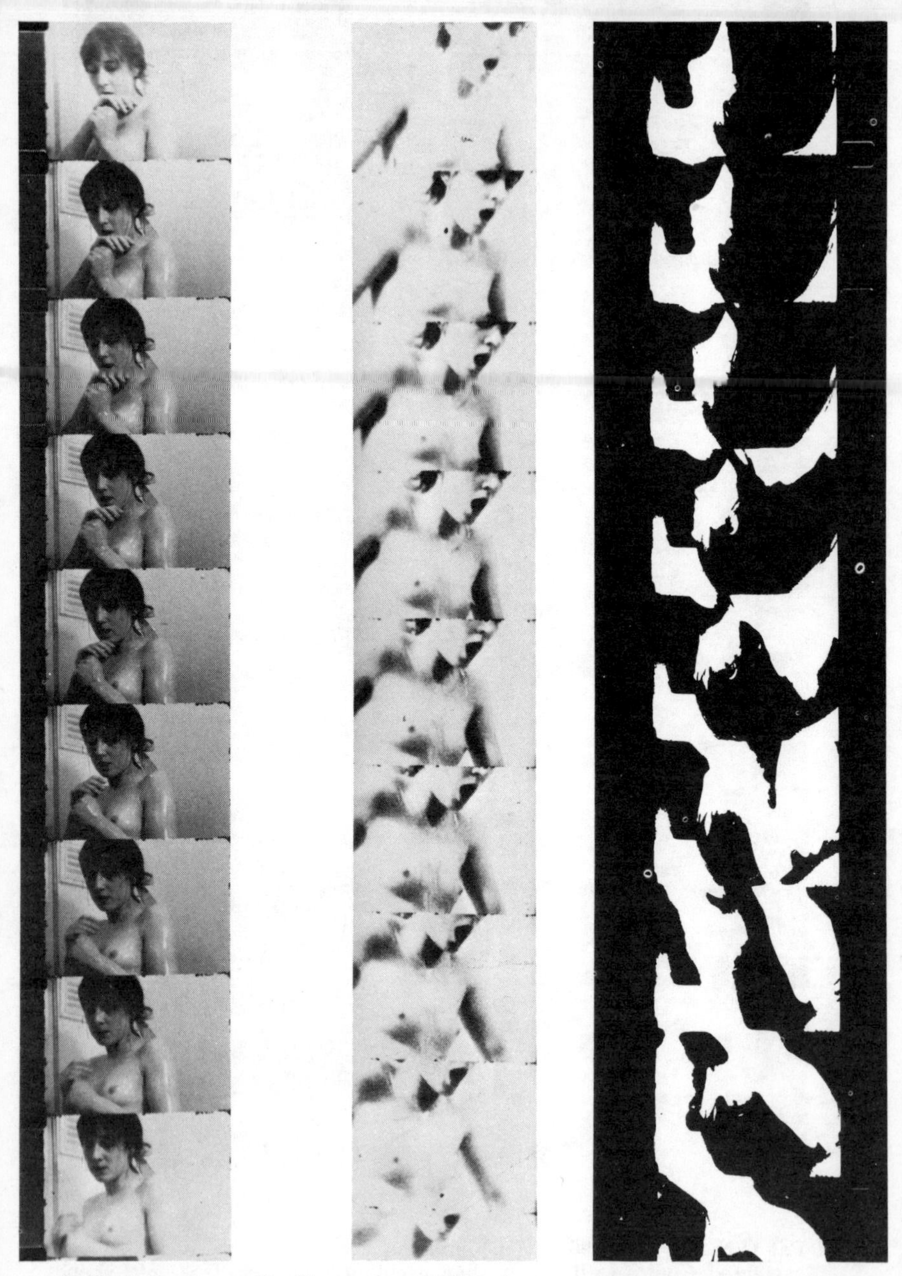

56 Fred Drummond's *Shower Proof* 1969: loop printing and increasing high contrast lead from sensuous full tonal range to virtual abstraction.

57 Scott Bartlett's *Metanomen* 1966: unresolved tensions in a boy–girl relationship are represented by the threatening (high-contrast) landscape that surrounds them.

58 Bartlett's *Moon 69* 1969: Bartlett uses some of the subtlest colour images ever created in an optical printer in a 'spiritual voyage across the impossible'.

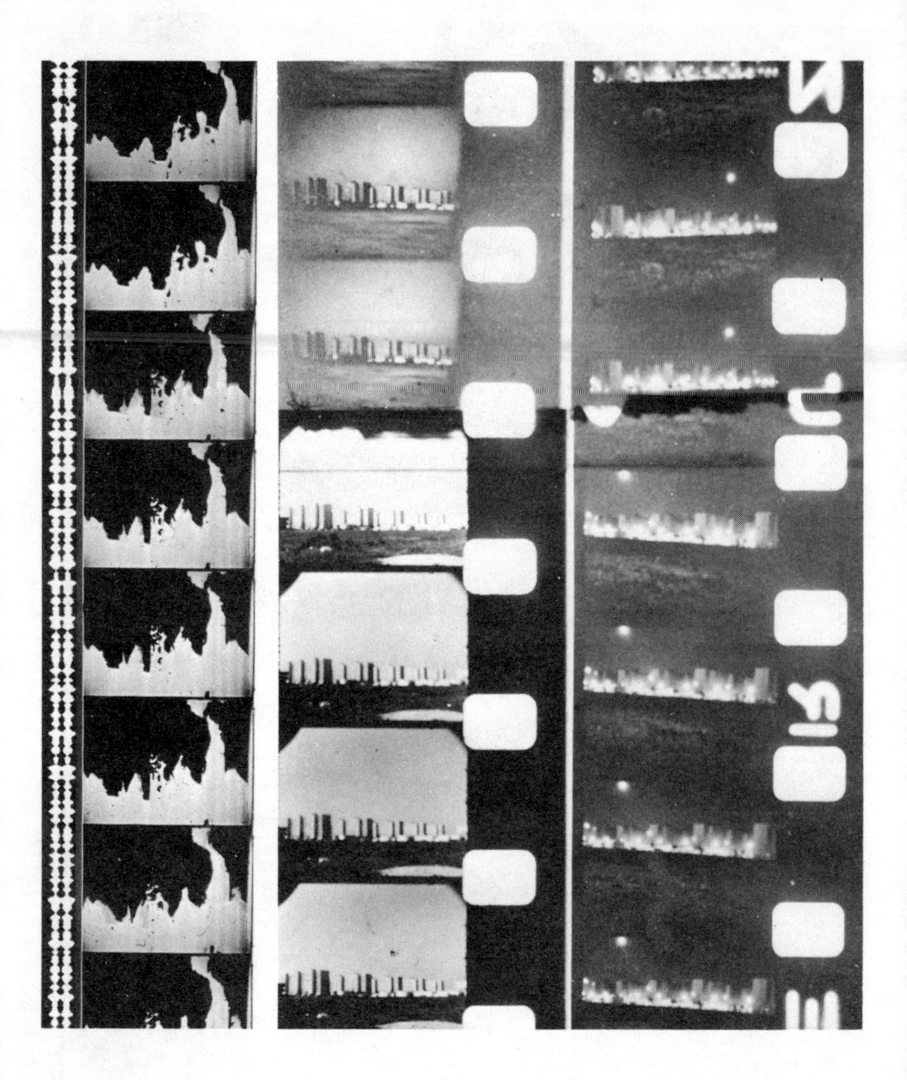

59 David Lourie's *Project One* 1968: Lourie rediscovers the images of his film by slowing them down and rephotographing them in a home-made optical printer.

60 Ulrich Hertzog's *Film Two Tiel 1* 1968: the image of a block of flats becomes the subject of an extended film essay.

61 Bruce Conner's *Vivian* 1964: sequential single-frame photography (pixillation almost) makes camera and girl dance together in Conner's collage portrait of Vivian Kurz.

62 Bruce Conner.

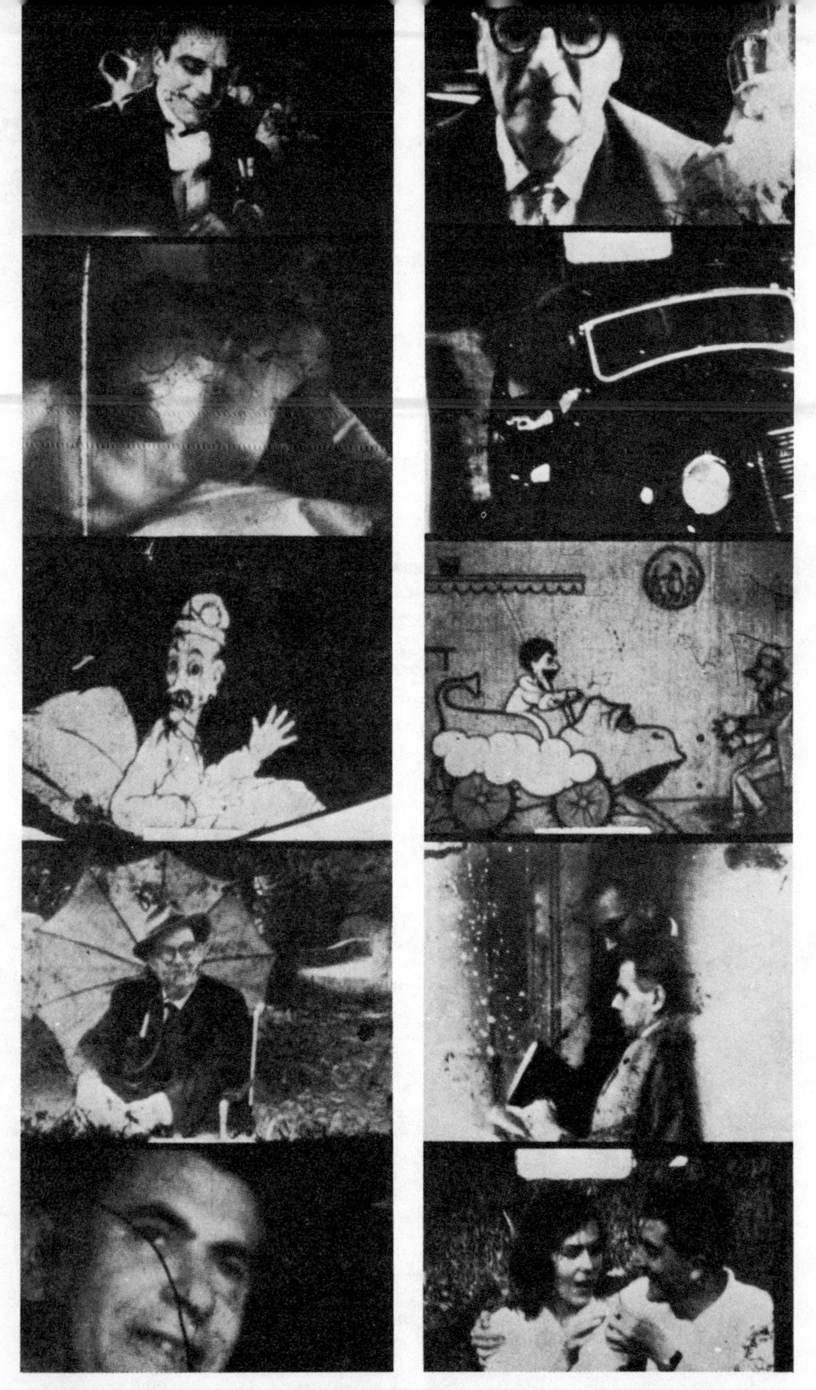

63 Victor and Silvio Loffredo's *Court Bouillon* 1952–62: a lovingly assembled single-frame film and photo collage.

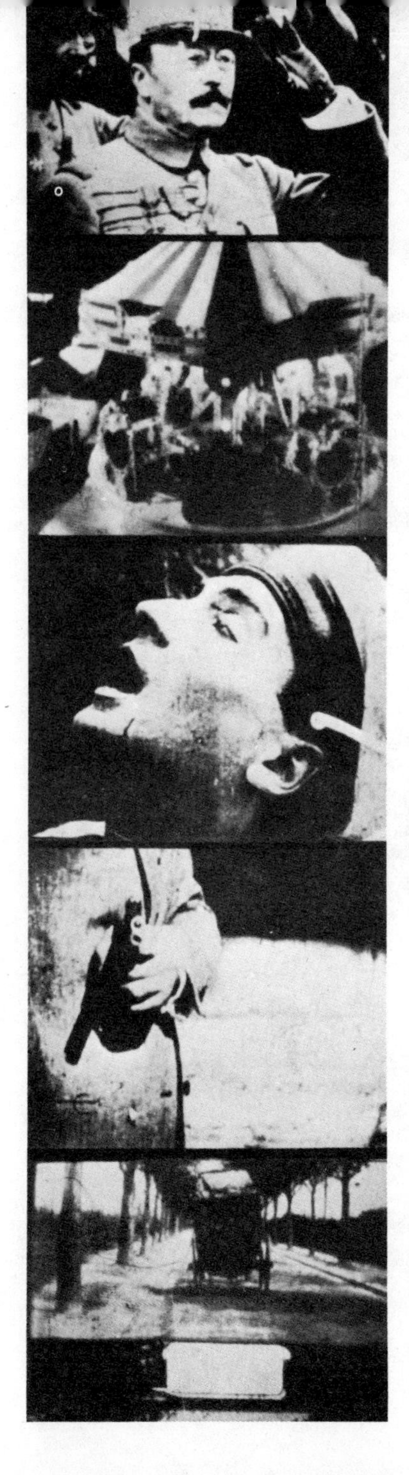
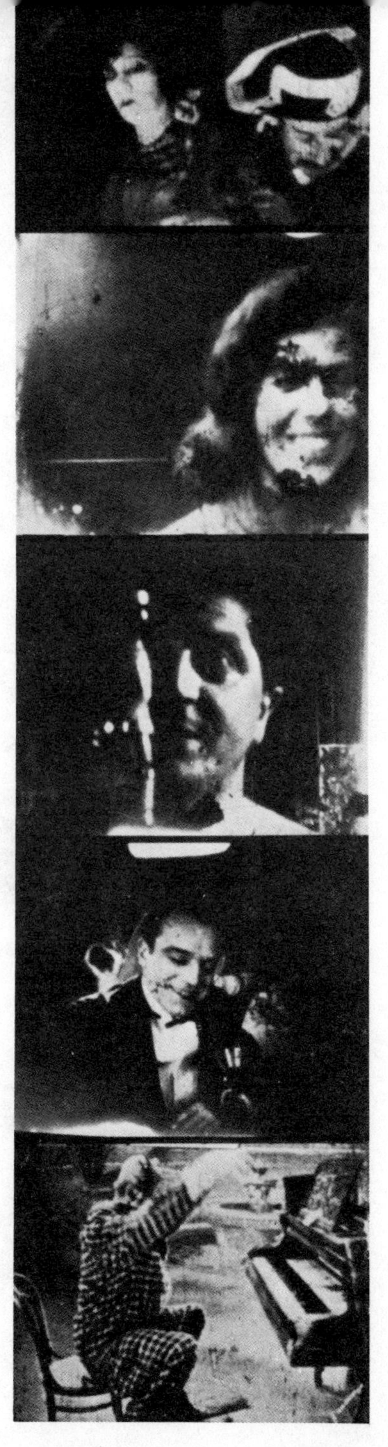

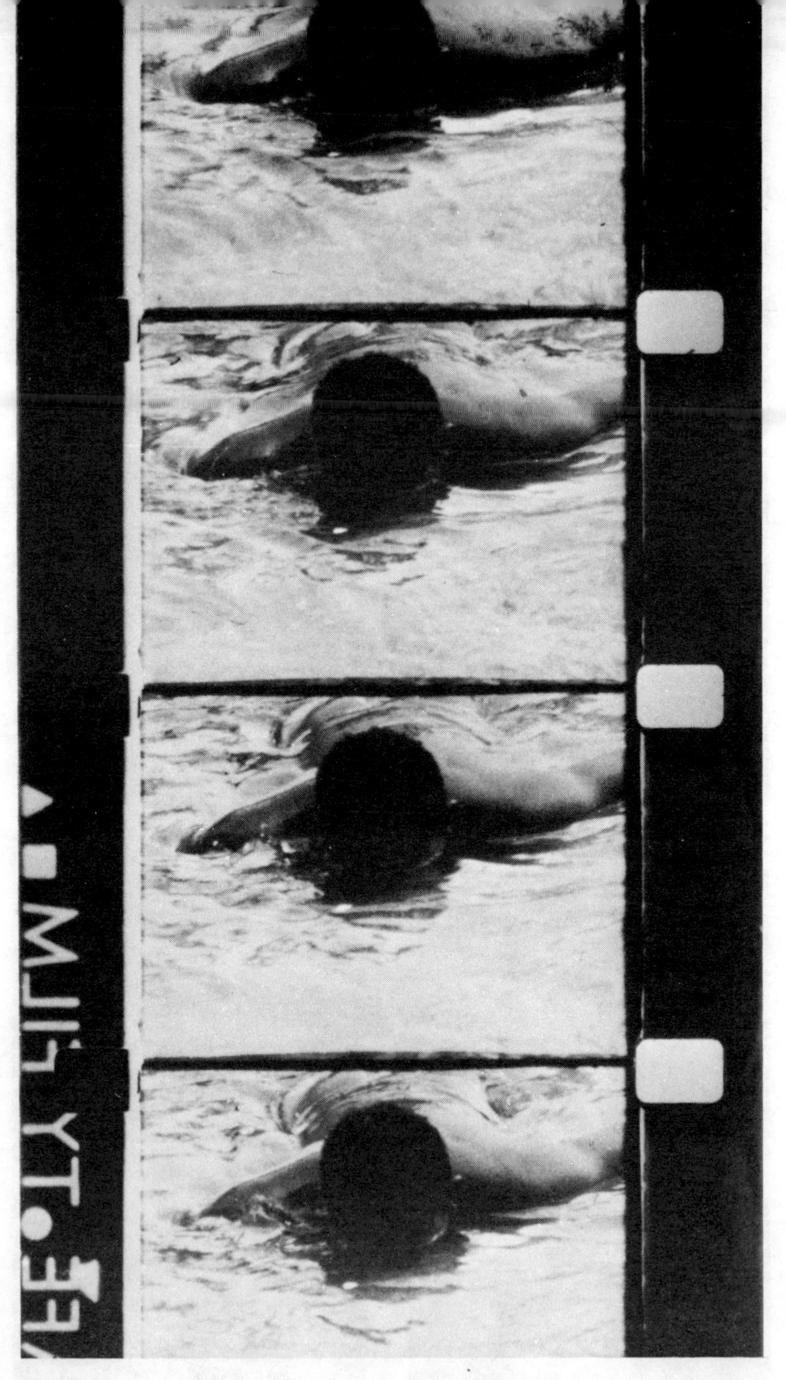

64 The final stage of Gianfranco Barucello's *Perforce* 1968.

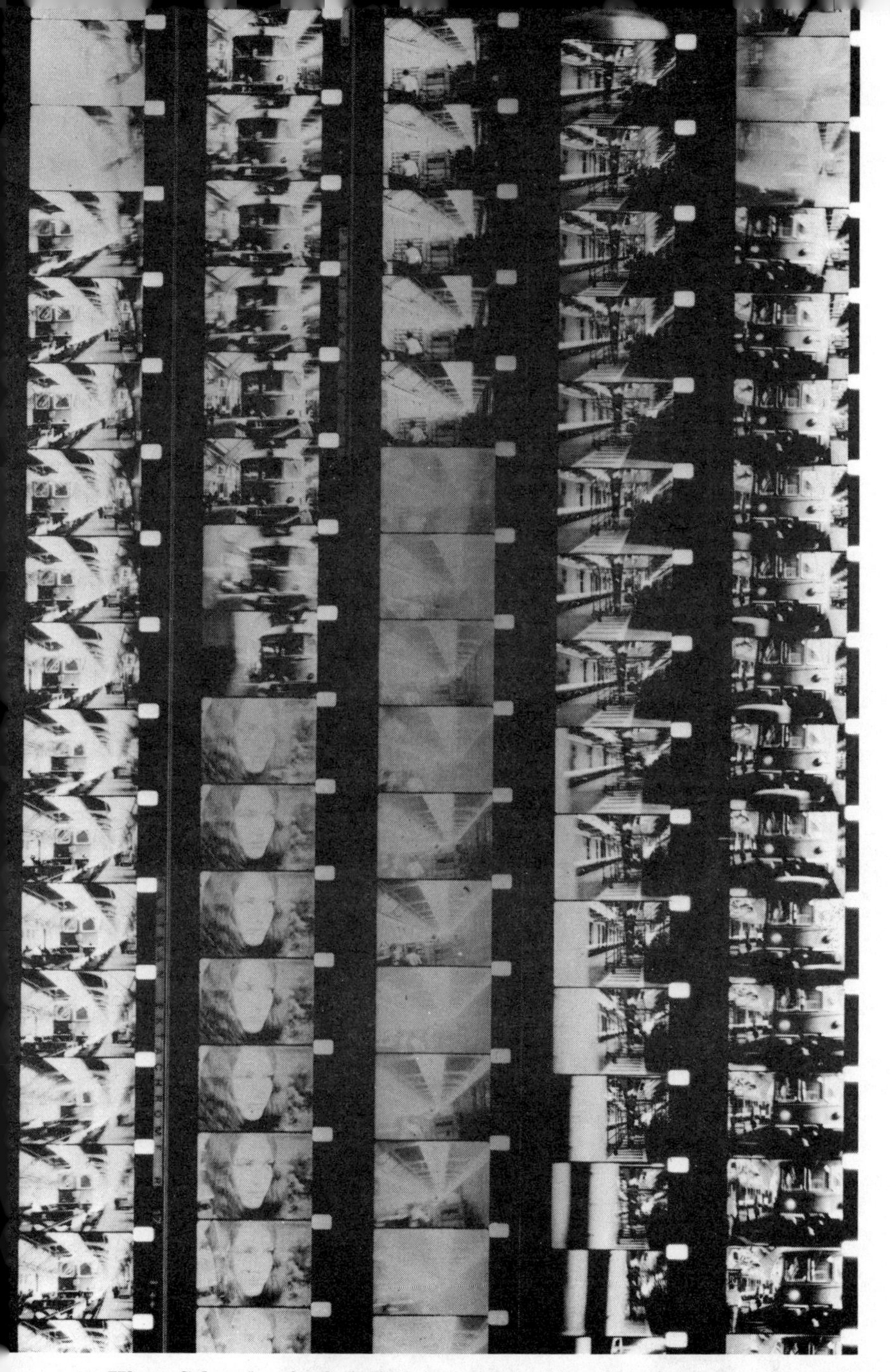

65 Klaus Schoenherr's *Gedanken beim Befuehlen einer Maedchenhaut* 1968 (literally meaning 'Thoughts while defiling a young girl's skin').

66 Schoenherr (self-portrait).

67 Alfredo Leonardi, prime mover of the Italian Film-makers' Co-op.

68 Alfredo Leonardi's *Book of the Saints of Eternal Rome* 1968 starring Pino Pascali.

69 Dore O in her own film *Alaska* 1968.

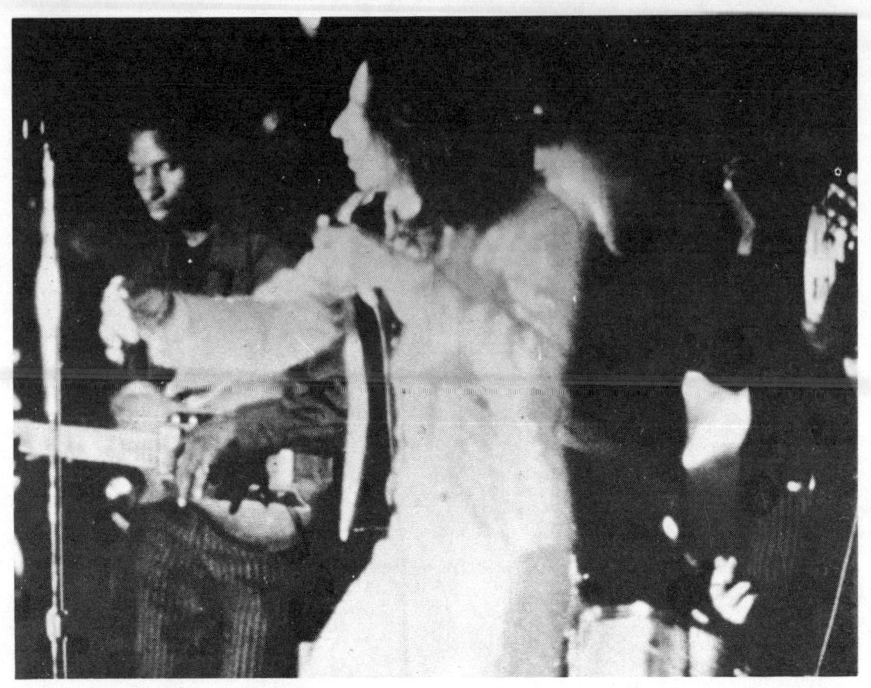

70 and 71 Warren Sonbert's *Where did our Love go?* 1966. The lower picture contains a portrait of the film-maker Andrew Meyer.

72 Jonas Mekas, film-maker and champion of the independent cinema, shooting in Central Park.

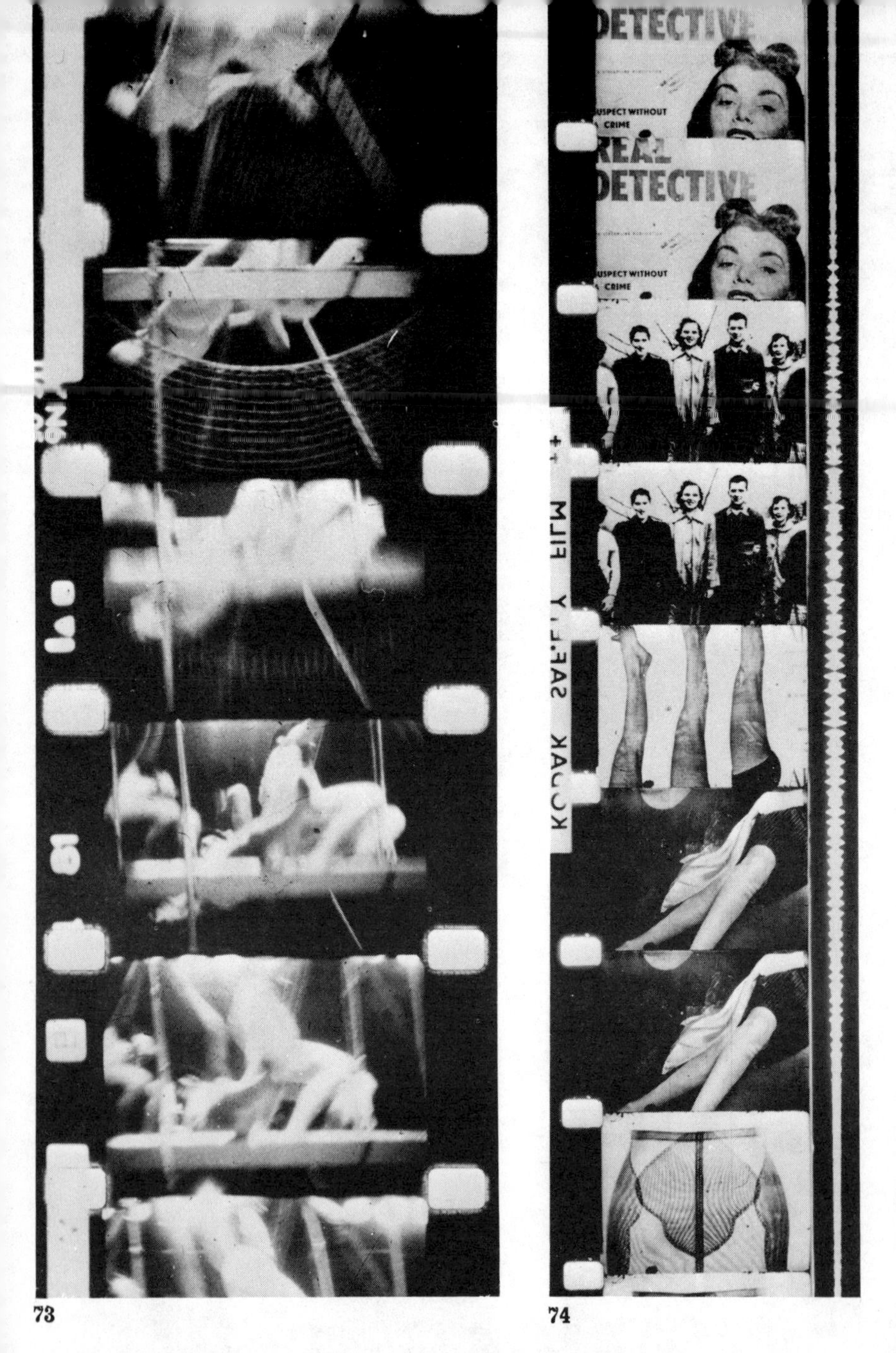

73 Frames from Jonas Mekas' *Circus Notebook* 1966.

74 Frames from *Marvo Movies* 1967–8 by Jeff Keen, father of the English independent movement.

75 Pierre Clementi (with camera).

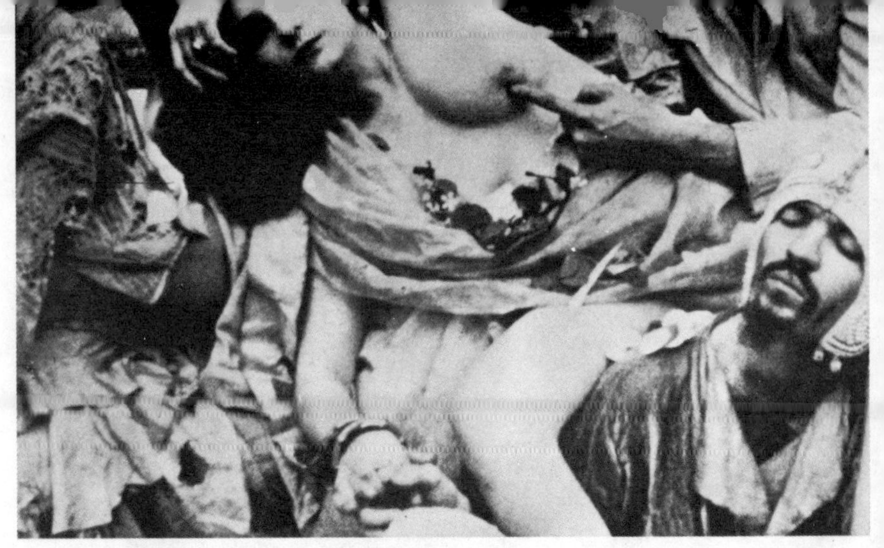

76 Jack Smith's *Flaming Creatures* 1963 was extensively banned on account of its exposure of limp male genitals. The beauty of Smith's film lies in its complete rejection of conventional (narrative) cinematography.

77 Ron Rice's *Chumlum* 1964: a frame from Rice's erotic masterpiece.

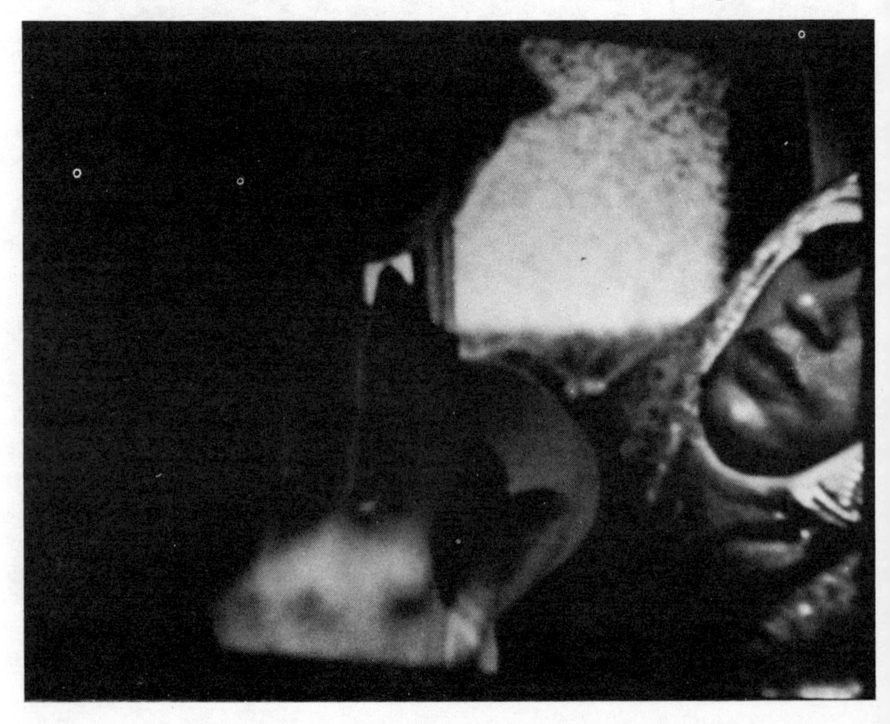

78 Etienne O'Leary.

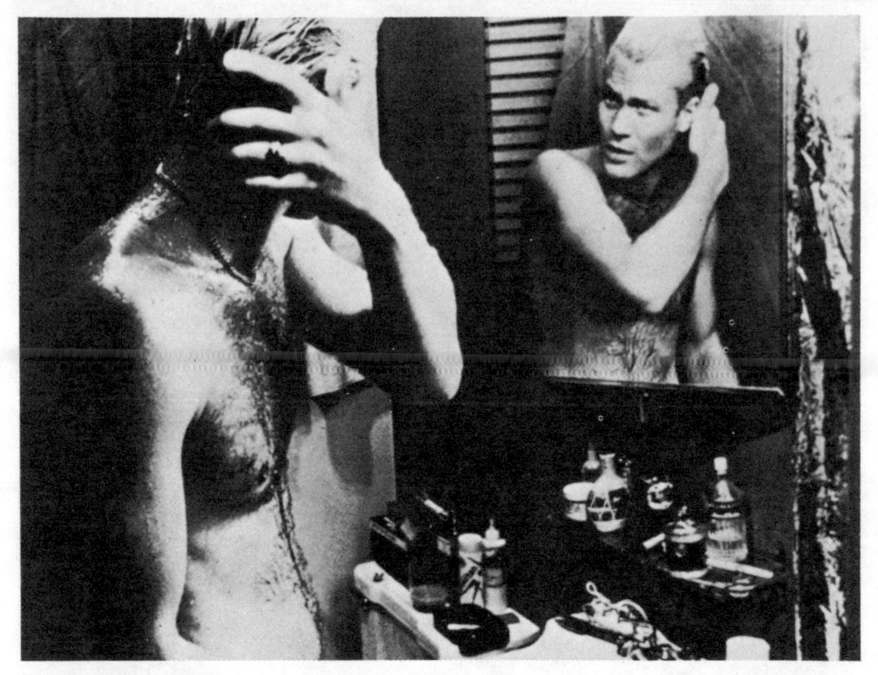

79 Andy Warhol's celebration of the star system: Paul America in *My Hustler* 1966.

80 Stars—Viva and Taylor Mead—in Warhol's *Lonesome Cowboys* 1967.

81 Valie Export in her own *Tapp und Tastfilm* 1968.

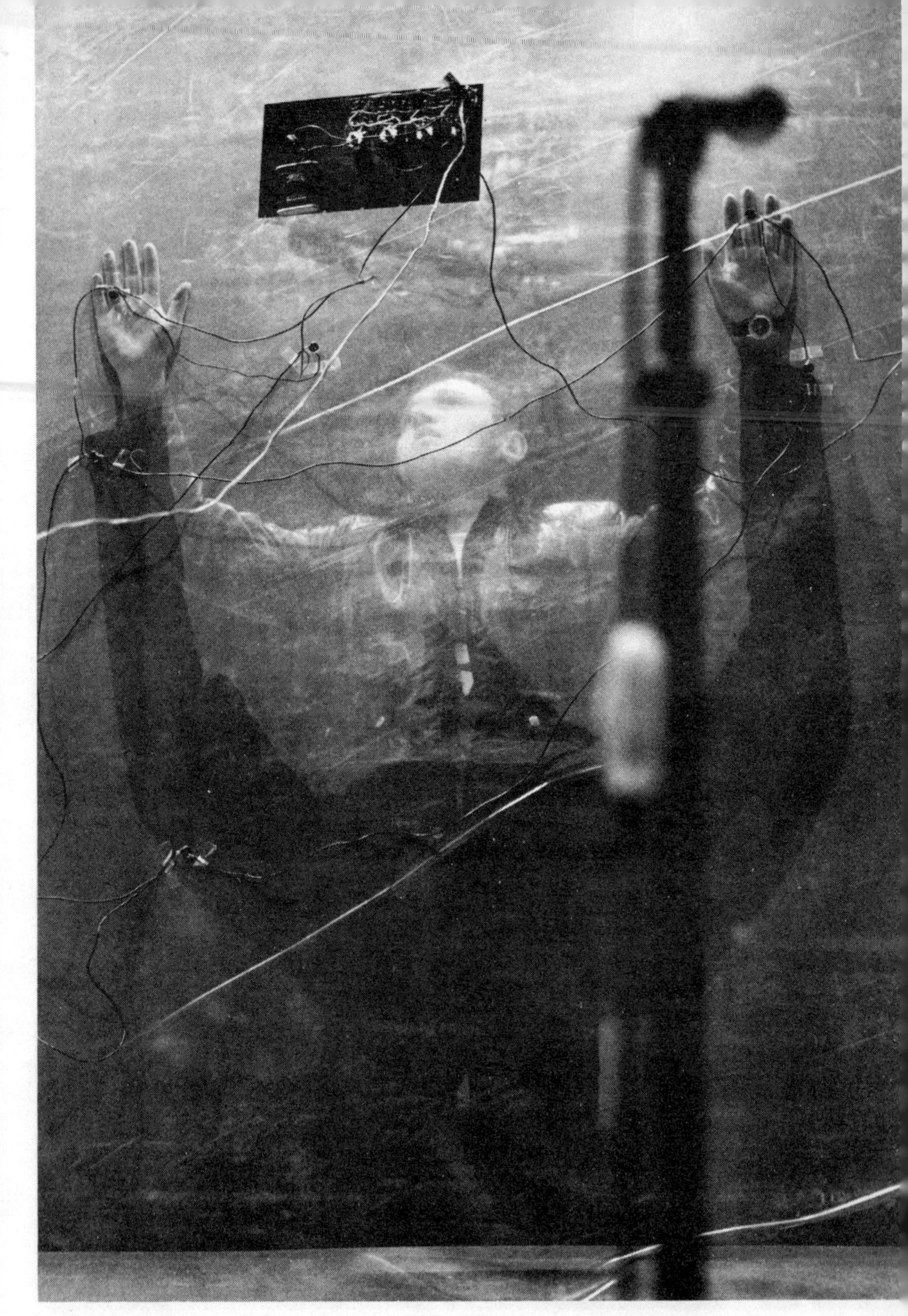

82 *Electron-ray Tube* 1969 by Valie Export and Peter Weibel.

83 *Cutting* 1969: a 'talkie' by Export.

84 *Fingerprint* 1968: a piece for drive-in cinema by Peter Weibel.

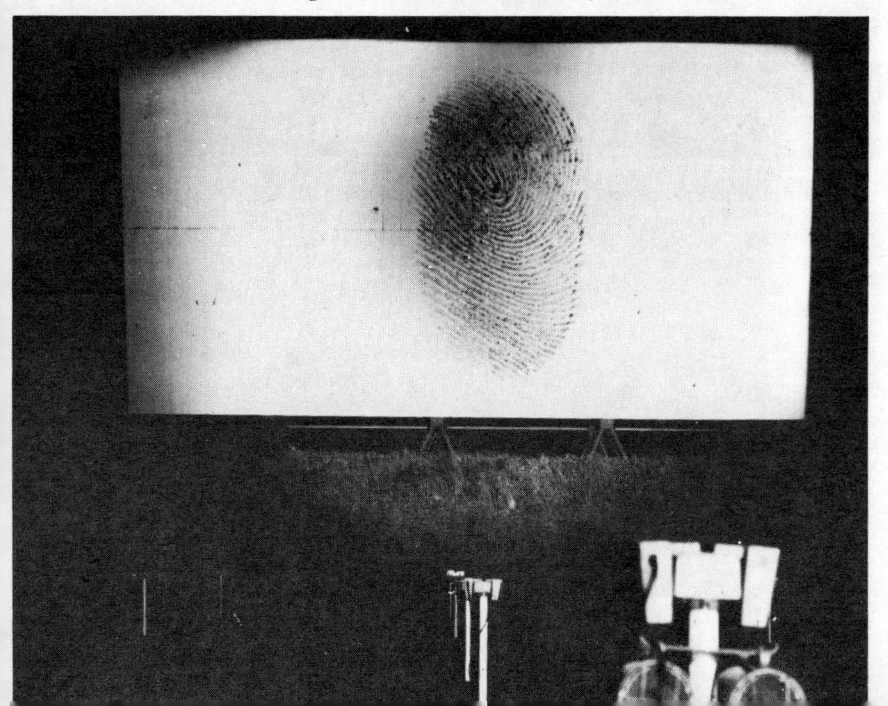

85 Rosa von Praunheim's *Sisters of the Revolution* 1968: 'a fighting gang of left-wing homosexuals who believe in the emancipation of women'.

86 An Otto Muehl *Materialaktion* (1965). Muehl's happenings also form the subject of a number of films by Kurt Kren.

87 Otto Muehl.

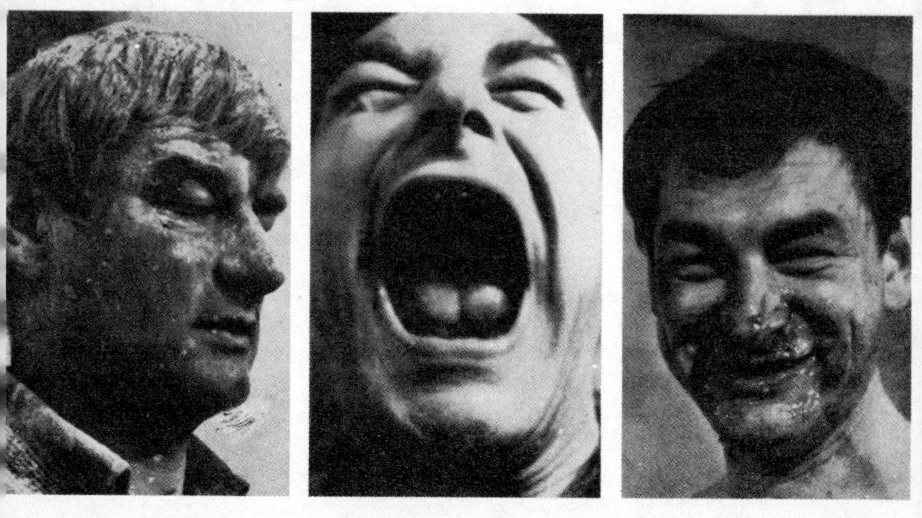

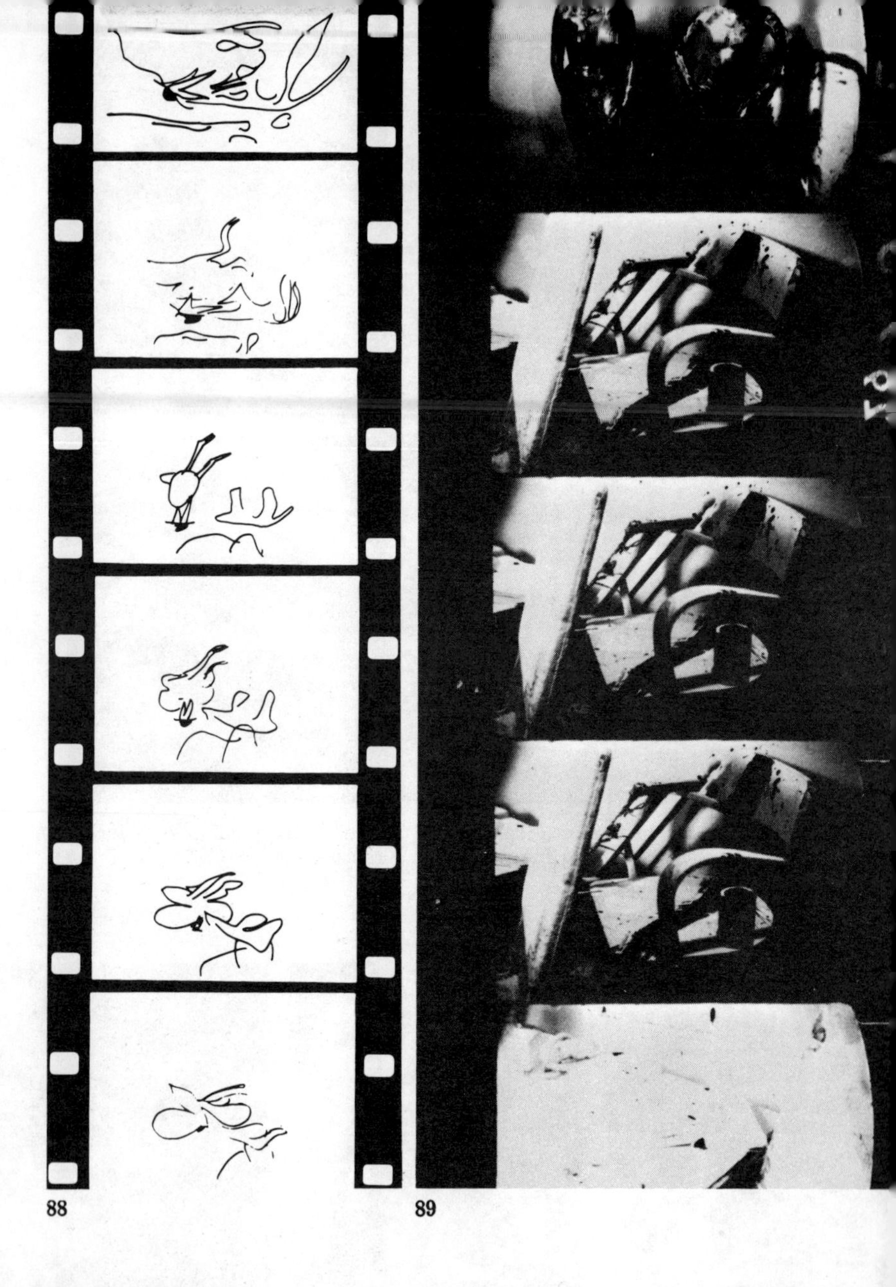

88

89

88 The emancipation of line drawing: Robert Breer's *A Man and his Dog out for Air* 1957.

89 Kurt Kren's *Ana Aktion Brus*.

90 Kurt Kren's *15/67 TV* 1967: a European (Austrian) anticipation of the American structural film.

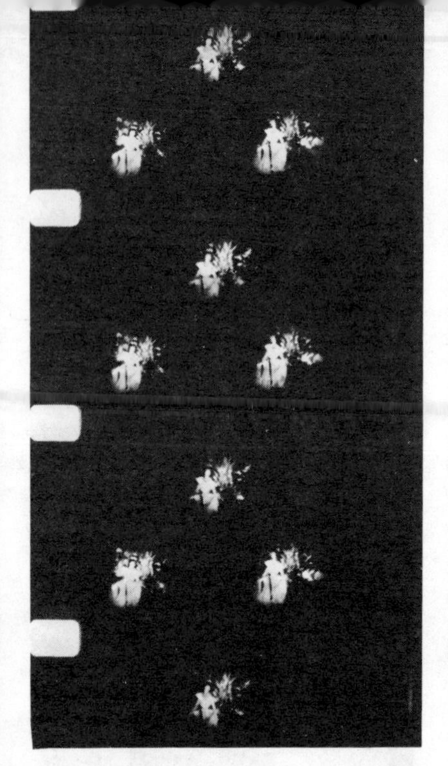
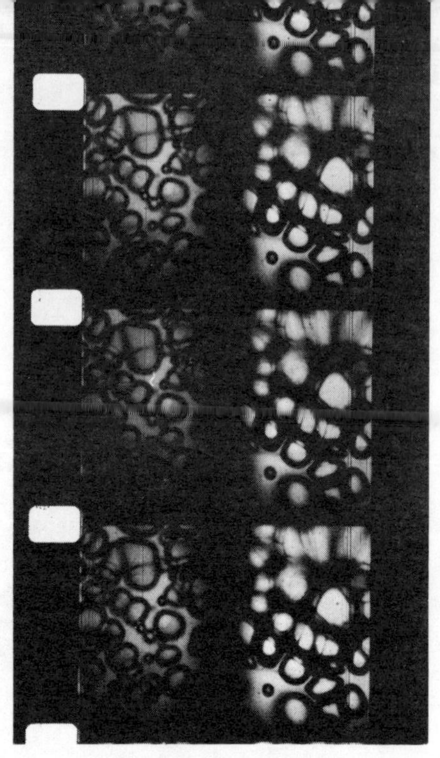

91, 92 The structural film: George Landow's *Bardo Follies* 1967: 'a paraphrasing of certain sections of the Bardo Thodol in motion picture terms'. Before becoming bubbles, the looped multiplying image is of a seated girl waving to a passing boat.

93 William and Birgit Hein's *Rohfilm* 1968, showing an 8mm image of William (physically) cut into a 16mm image of Cologne Cathedral.

94 The structural film: Paul Sharits' *Peace Mandala/End War* 1967.

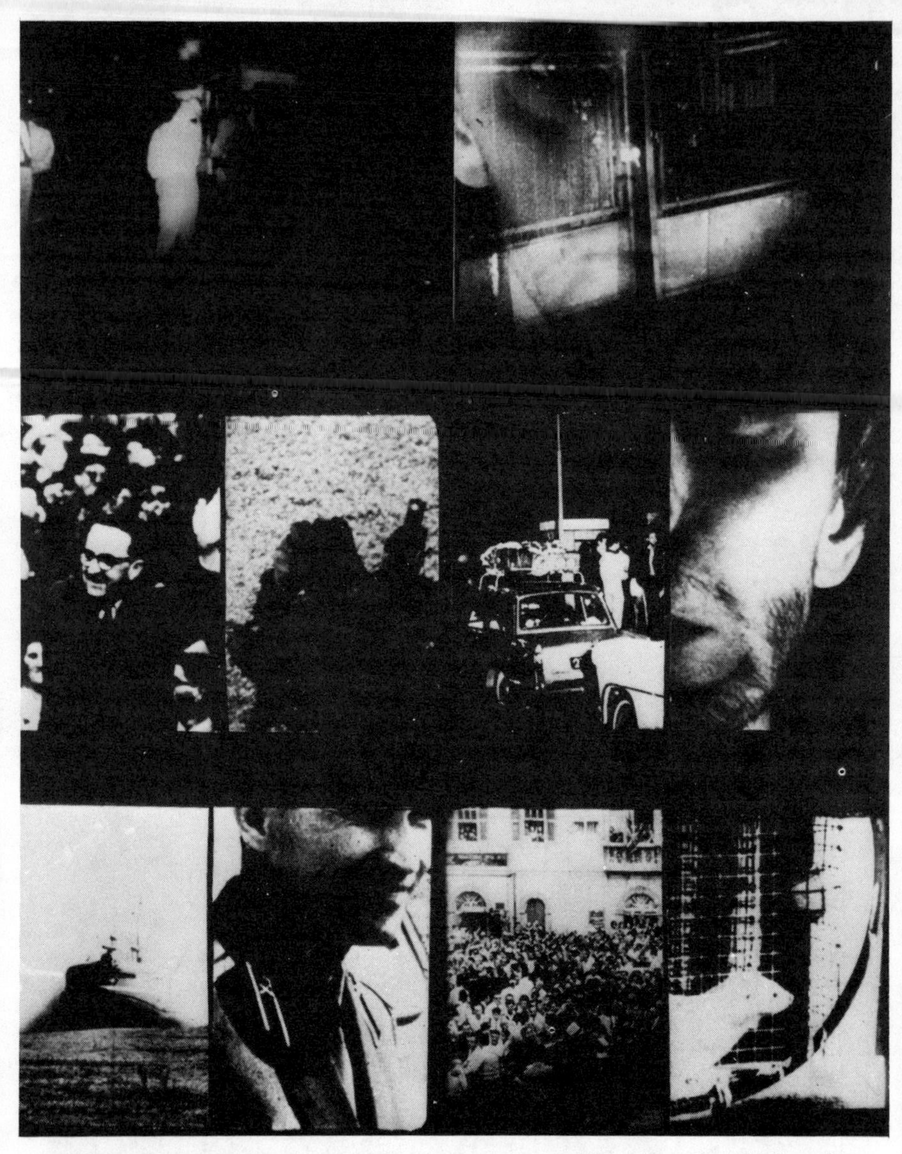

95 Malcolm Le Grice's *Castle 2* 1968: a two-screen film collage in which each screen divides itself.

96 William and Birgit Hein's *Work in Progress* 1969–70.

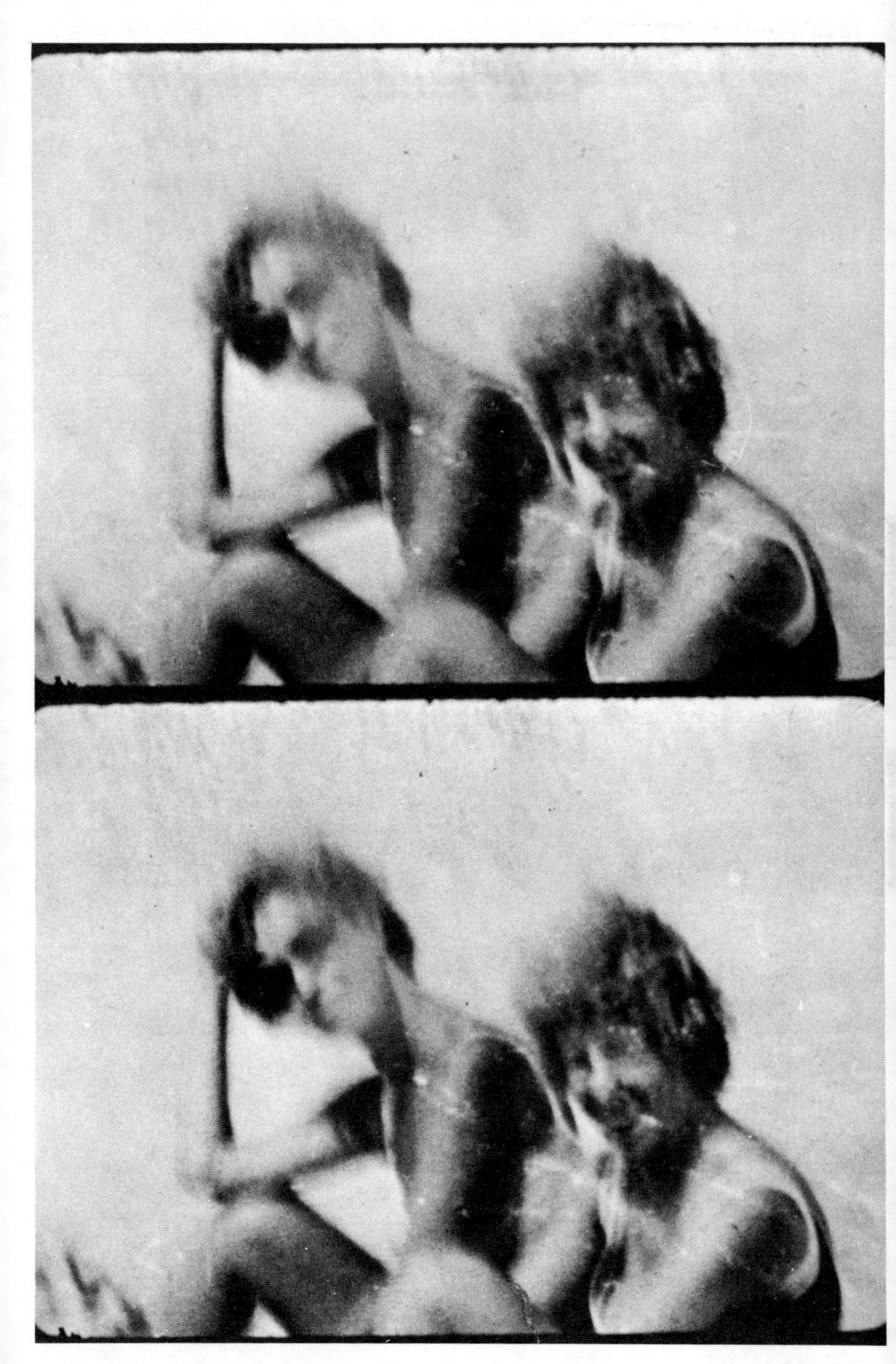

97 Lutz Mommartz' *Eisenbahn* 1967 (top), and *Selbstschusse* 1967, a moving self-portrait dance.

98 Joyce Wieland's *La Raison avant la Passion* 1969: the face is that of Pierre Trudeau.

99 Albie Thoms' *Bolero* 1967.

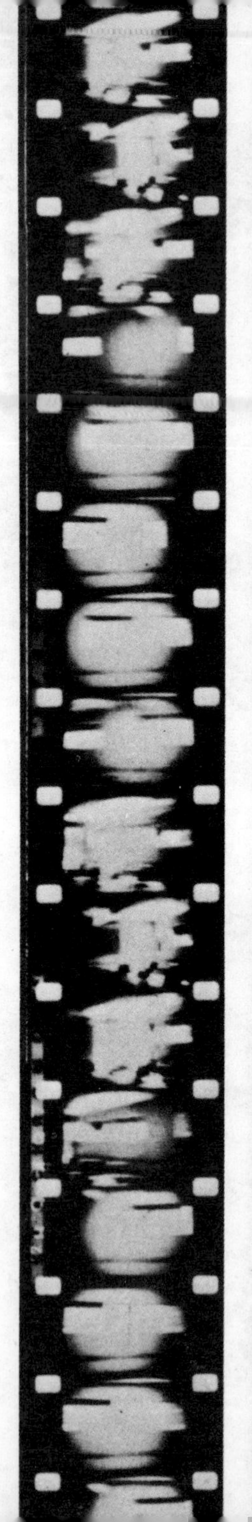

100 The structural film: Mike Snow's ⟷ 1969: a classroom is seen in increasingly rapid left-to-right, then up-and-down, pans.

The co-operative movement—internationalism—new directions

The choice by post-war American film-makers of the amateur's gauge, 16 mm, was an important one, for by doing so they consciously cut themselves off from all but non-theatrical exhibition. However, this gesture of defiant independence from the film industry laid open to them the rapidly increasing number of college film societies—the much discussed 'college circuit' which stands today about 9000 strong. The potential of this circuit could not be fully realized, however, until some means was found of distributing a greater proportion of the new films being made.

In New York, Cinema 16, the Gryphon Group and some commercial distributors were accepting new work but they exercised increasing moral/aesthetic discrimination in their selection. In 1957 Bob Pike founded an explicitly for-the-film-makers by-the-film-makers distribution/exhibition service in Los Angeles, which acted for a number of years as the main outlet for West Coast film-makers. Wallace Berman, Curtis Harrington, John and James Whitney, Ray and Charles Eames and Oskar Fischinger were the founder members. Pike accepted films for distribution on a percentage of rental basis or bought them outright, making him in effect a quasi-commercial organization. In San Francisco, film-maker Bruce Baillie, recently back from Europe, began a series of free screenings for the Bay area in 1961, which led to the development of the Canyon Cinema Co-op in 1966. In New York, Jonas Mekas, under whose editorship *Film Culture* (founded in 1955) had become the unofficial voice of the new movement, responded to the unsung challenge of the non-distributed East Coast film-makers by starting screenings at the Charles Theatre and founding the New York Film-makers' Co-operative in 1962.

The charter of this Co-op was quite revolutionary. It guaranteed distribution to any film-maker who submitted a print, and established the unprecedented return of seventy-five per cent of the rental fee, a figure set by the film-maker himself. Its impact was immediate: an audience was suddenly available to film-makers who had been working, unheard of in many cases, for several years (the Kuchar brothers since 1954, Ken Jacobs and Jack Smith since 1956, Harry Smith since the early forties, etc.), and new film-makers seemed to spring up overnight. More important, the Co-op's link with an exhibition outlet (first the

Charles Theatre, then the Film-makers' Cinemathèque), and with journals (*Film Culture* and the *Newsletter*) made it possible for film-makers to become known to an important public almost immediately; some, like Warhol, were recognized with their first films. It was no longer essential to wait ten years for critical acclaim.

SHORT FILM CRAFTSMEN

In 1960, in *Film Culture 20*, Jonas Mekas, already anticipating the emergence of American independent film-making, gave a list of the significant new film-makers working at the time. His list included: Joseph Strick (*The Savage Eye*); Lionel Rogosin (*Come Back Africa*); John Cassavetes (*Shadows*); Robert Frank and Alfred Leslie (*Pull My Daisy*); Maya Deren (*The Very Eye of Night*); Charles Boultenhouse (*Hand Written*); Bert Stern (*Jazz on a Summer's Day*); Shirley Clarke (*The Connection*) as well as himself and his brother Adolfas (*Guns of the Trees*).

The complete list, although omitting most of the 'underground' film-makers Mekas was to meet during the next two or three years, was still intelligent and perceptive for its time, recording the significant change in the aspirations of semi-professional film-makers during the late fifties, especially in the New York area.

These film-makers, while fully accepting the traditional craftsmanship of film production, often to the extent of working with a complete camera crew, etc., aimed to bring new subject matter and a new directness of approach to the cinema. Partly inspired by the kitchen-sink realists in England, and partly by hints of the New Wave to come in France, their movement was, in effect, more of an attempt to revitalize the existing commercial cinema than to provide anything that could be called an alternative.

When the 'complete alternative' presented itself as a well-established fact (in the form of the New York Film-makers Co-operative and the so-called college circuit of exhibition outlets) in the mid-sixties, the position of feature film-makers on Jonas Mekas' list became clearer. Shirley Clarke and Jonas Mekas moved towards the Co-op (which they had both been instrumental in setting up); Strick and Cassavetes moved back towards the commercial cinema, which in turn was already moving towards them.

However, the semi-professional film-maker craftsman still very much persisted, providing the more traditional film critics with their one and only point of reference in the whole 'underground'. Their work ranged from the cinepoem (in the tradition of Weinberg and Maas) such as Charles Boultenhouse's *Hand Written*

(1959), to visual studies in the Ralph Steiner and 'city symphony' tradition, such as Francis Thomson's *NY, NY* (1957).

Boultenhouse's *Hand Written*, a nine-minute film, makes very rich use of the counterpoint between image—meticulously-constructed shots of a man at a table drinking a cocktail—and the spoken Mallarmé poem on the soundtrack. The man is both, literally, the film-maker and the 'poet'; the verbal images evolve separately, together they form the complete metaphor for the creative process—which is the subject of the poem.

At the other extreme, Thomson's *NY, NY* (plate 44) is a classic of its kind. Distorting reflective surfaces break up the New York skyline into abstracted moving shapes. Later, working with Alexander Hammid (Maya Deren's ex-partner), Thomson was responsible for the popular film success of the New York World Fair of 1964 with their multiscreen (three 35-mm) film *To Be Alive*, made for the Johnson's Wax Pavilion. Such sponsored projects became increasingly offered to 'craftsman' film-makers.

During the fifties and the first half of the sixties, the dance film (interpretations of the work of the great American choreographers of the period) provided material for a number of these film-artists. Many took their starting point from Maya Deren whose last film *The Very Eye of Night* (1958), a work beautifully designed to be shown in its negative state, set standards for every dance film that followed. Shirley Clarke's *Dance in the Sun* (1953) with Daniel Nagrin was particularly indebted to Deren's *A Study in Choreography for Camera*. Other such dance films were: Shirley Clarke's *Bullfight* (1955) and *Moment in Love* (1957), both with Anna Sokolow; Ed Emshwiller's *Dance Chromatic* (1959), *Lifelines* (1960), *Totem* (1963) and *Fusion* (1963) (*Totem* and *Fusion* both with the Alwin Nicolais Dance Company, *Fusion* sponsored by the Spring Mills Company to promote their linen); Stan Vanderbeek's *Sight* (1965) with Bob Morris and Carolee Schneemann, *Spherical Space* (1966) with Elaine Summers and *Room Service* (1965) with Yvonne Rainer; and Hilary Harris' classical *Nine Variations on a Dance Theme* (1967).

In *Dance Chromatic* (plate 45), Ed Emshwiller, science-fiction illustrator and professional feature film cameraman, choreographed a dancer's movements with the thick brushstrokes of an abstract expressionist painting, superimposing the two actions/activities alternately in-camera. He was motivated partly by the belief that action painting should 'exist in time' and partly by a desire to 'mix incompatibles'. *Lifelines* similarly combines the poses of a model with moving (animated) drawings. A mixed media piece, *Bodyworks* (1965–) involved four live dancers, three portable (hand-held) projectors, three portable screens, a fragmentation mirror (to split up images) and five projectionists. It was a further development of the theme, the projected images revealing and transforming the dancers' movements. Emshwiller's basic preoccupation with 'graphic' imagery is continued in the two more recent feature-length films he has made: *Relativity* (1966) and *Image, Flesh and Voice* (1969; plate 46). Both are highly cinematic (and too well-known to justify description here), but are dominated by a clear sense of visual composition; different from the 'composition' taught in art schools obviously, since it involves movement, but directly corresponding in its respect for pleasing relationships on screen.

Another film by Shirley Clarke, *Bridges Go Round* (1958; plate 47), a study of 'the patterns made by bridges in space, their massive power, and the *particular quality of motion that is given to bridges when moving in relation to them*' (my italics), set new standards for the Ralph Steiner school. Though she used multiple printing to remove the images from their immediately recognizable context, Mrs Clarke does not simply make 'abstractions'—she multiplies one's awareness of the bulk and relative movements within the structures. Scott Bartlett's *Metanomen* (1966) is the obvious film to compare with Shirley Clarke's (Bartlett would strongly resist being classified as a semi-professional film-craftsman, though, as in the work of most of the West Coast optical school, craftsmanship is essential to his working process). For *Metanomen* is also dominated by the physical structure of a bridge, but already in this—his first work—Bartlett is more concerned with the interpretation of images as they contribute to the kinetic structure of the film than with revealing (by description, montage or whatever) their original function or purpose. *His* girders (shown in extreme high contrast) are shadow patterns providing a 'context' in which to state the boy/girl relationship central to the film (plate 57).

Stan Vanderbeek's dance pieces are something of a rarity in his work, but in his approach to film-making he is very much a subscriber to the 'professionalism' of the craftsman film-maker. Vanderbeek started making animated collage films during the mid-fifties, using cut-out and reproduced photographic images, and representational or abstract paint or ink drawings. His subjects range from the absurd to the tragi-comic, sometimes deadly serious (as in *Breathdeath* 1963; plate 48), sometimes pure anarchy (as in *Dance of the Looney Spoons* 1965). Vanderbeek, almost more than any other contemporary film-maker, is obsessed with technology and he has made a serious attempt to bring the computer, television and all the essential communications media within the range of the film artist. *Spherical Space*, a dance film, is one of his simplest uses of 'hardware'—in this case a 195-degree camera lens—and one of his most successful. The image of a naked girl, dancing *with* the camera in a wood, her limbs and the tree trunks being sucked towards the centre of the screen, is quite breathtaking. He has not always been so successful. His project to establish an international image theatre, based upon a series of satellite-linked Movie-Dromes (each being both contributor and receiver), is still not completely satisfactorily worked out, even after six years of work on the prototype. But the problems are only minor technical ones (mainly concerned with excess reflected light). The premise is still a very exciting one: the audience sit or lie beneath a dome on which is projected a vast flow of images (as in the *Vortex Concerts*), the images in this case being called either from immediate reality (live) or from film/video libraries attached to the dome, the common denominator being their ability to 'inspire basic intuitive instincts of self realization'. Presentations could range from a complete cultural history of western civilization to an explanation in microscopic terms of the workings of the bloodstream. But these subjects would be shown as never before, in a non-verbal, visually self-explanatory image language. How much of the multiple imagery the viewer took in would be up to him, and the experience, therefore, uniquely his.

Vanderbeek's work with computers, which has occupied most of the past five years, has resulted in *Computer Art* (*number one*) (1966) and the *Poemfield* series (plate 49). Although only one of this recent series is presently available for viewing, it is sufficient to demonstrate Vanderbeek's very tactile response to the computer's image-generating potential.

William Hindle has earned himself the reputation of being the most consummate artist-technician working on the West Coast today. Involved in film since the late thirties (when he was a child bit-part player), he began making personal films in 1957. He has supported himself by working extensively for television (CBS and Westinghouse), which has probably contributed to his technical mastery. His best-known works are *29 Merci Merci* (1966), *FFFTCM* (*Fan Fare for the Common Man* 1967), *Chinese Firedrill* and *Billabong* (both 1968) and *Watersmith* (1969). The unifying factor in his work is the exceptional polish of his image-flow, which he achieves despite the extreme ambiguity of their content. Bartlett's films have the same smooth appearance, but his images are selected for precisely that effect—Hindle manages to combine disturbing apparent opposites.

Billabong, for example, opens with a deceptively simple sequence of shots establishing a location—a road leading to an apparently deserted barrack-like building—photographed as in a conventional (well-made) documentary (less its commentary). The film then becomes increasingly manic—the images more awkward and darker, slowly increasing in contrast and losing their natural colour. The building is inhabited by young men, who show no apparent reason for living. They sit, grin, play cards, touch themselves, but never leave, never look out even. As the contrast increases, acidic colour filters are superimposed—detachment from reality indicated clinically through a formal device. ('Billabong' is Australian for a stream diverted into a stagnant pool; the barracks are, in fact, some kind of a reform school work camp.) To make its final point, the camera approaches an open window, and there, directly outside (in full colour again), is the Pacific Ocean.

Bruce Baillie worked briefly for Will Hindle at one time early in his career and shares something of Hindle's technical perfectionism. Baillie, founder of the Canyon Cinema Co-op, is one of the West Coast's most complete film-makers. He started to make films in the early sixties, making 'news' items 'for a specific local audience'—the audience in the Bay area who came to his Canyon screenings. At this time, his films were strictly narrative or documentary, edited only to restore sequence and continuity. *To Parsifal* (1963) was his first major work, a film poem to summer, structured on the Parsifal legend—huge seascapes, fishermen, railwaymen laying tracks through tall grassland, a clear life-supporting mountain stream, a vision of a girl. Baillie begins to edit with an epic sense, conveying a growing awareness of a larger meaning to the work being done—both to the labourers' work in the film and to his own film-making process. In *Mass for the Dakota Sioux* (1964), a film about life extinction but hinting at escape, he acknowledges the potential in 'imperfect' imagery—over-exposed shots, 'awkward' camera movements and editing—for conveying direct emotive meaning (urgency, exhaustion, tension, etc.). His work continuously moves between the epic and the highly intuitive, as the subject dictates. *Quixote* (1965–6) is a feature-length work and Baillie's most committed and complex social statement. Essentially, it is a composition of open observations and often bitter reflections made on a journey across America, using dynamic superimpositions—shots of Vietcong warfare over shots of New York, for example—not for propagandist reasons, but because the combined image externalizes the practised hostility of that particular environment. *Quixote* was also the turning point in Baillie's film-making. Since then his main films have developed along a restrained, more formal course, though when the occasion demands, he is still committed to making documentaries—like *Newsreel* (1966).

Tung (1966), 'a poem to a friend named Tung', is an uninterrupted flow of superb colour images—a girl in negative (walking) floating on a field of moving colours—while a poem appears, almost as punctuation, across the bottom of the frame. *Castro Street* (1966; plates 50 and 51) is an essay in the structure of images. Baillie marries colour images of one side of an industrial street ('female') with black and white of the other ('male'), using black-gloved hands as a flexible matte in front of the lens while shooting—filling in the dark areas with other images later. The picture quality and colour control he has achieved in this film has no equal in the commercial cinema—it is of the same quality as the very best work of Markopoulos, Hindle or Emshwiller.

In *Still Life* (1966) and *All My Life* (1966), Baillie condenses, with an almost classical Japanese discipline, a complete statement into a single shot. *Still Life* shows a table top, flowers and a few objects on it, a room with windows at the far end out of focus behind it, from a static camera position. A woman crosses one way, then returns; men's voices are heard talking. It takes two minutes in all. *All My Life* is a single pan across a fence with roses, and up to the sky (crossed with a telegraph wire). Ella Fitzgerald sings the title song, *All my Life* . . . These two films represent Baillie's most powerful affirmation of the purpose of cinematography. Baillie's most recent work is *Quick Billy* (1968–).

Ron Finne's *How Old Is the Water* (1968) could have been a version of Steiner's *H_2O*, but absolutely isn't. Finne's film does not attempt to manipulate surface reflections into abstractions; instead it reveals the dynamics of water movement (over a small waterfall) with almost a naturalist's insight. Finne's is a film of rushing and falling—the water tracing paths of light on the screen as in Anger's Vermeer-like *Eaux d'Artifice*. Finne draws attention to the empathy that exists between humans and natural rhythms by his brilliant choice of soundtrack—the hypnotic, repetitive sound of a Red Indian 'hand game' and chant.

Steve Dwoskin is perhaps the most traditional of all the film-maker craftsmen. A New Yorker now in London, Dwoskin's films contain no superimpositions, no impulsive camera movements, no abstract images of any sort. They are conventional documentaries—even to the extent in one case of having a narration on the soundtrack. They are experimental only in their uncompromising commitment to their subject matter—the study of human isolation and the gestures we make towards communication. In his most famous film, *Alone* (1966; plate 52), the camera watches from two or three chosen positions, as a girl, lying on a bed, communicates her loneliness through her body. (To say she masturbates—which is how the film is often described—is an overstatement; she just expresses a desperate need for tactile response.) In *Me Myself and I* (1968), he records the evasion games and moments of vulnerability revealed by two people trapped together in a bathroom. Again, the trapping is not significant. We behave the same way towards each other almost all the time—the bathroom is Dwoskin's *Huis Clos,* a formal device that insists that participants and spectators confront their predicament. In *Chinese Checkers* (1967) and *Take Me* (1969), Dwoskin's camera takes a subjective view in a relationship. Two girls are playing Chinese checkers, but the real game is the one they are playing with each other. The camera cuts between them, becoming involved in their erotic swaying movements, watching as they become more and more embellished in each other's eyes (in erotic, grotesque make-up), until they lock in a passionate kiss. The camera in *Take Me* has a more ambiguous role. A girl directly tries to seduce it, giving a 'come on' to the audience, and the camera responds; but the relationship is peculiar, the girl retires from a kiss with her mouth smeared with paint. She persists, slowly becoming covered with paint. The relationship, and the film, ends when the painting activity is 'complete'. It is as though both the audience and the girl are being punished for their complicity in a (mutual) vicarious sexual relationship.

OPTICALS—FILM AS FILM AND FOUND FOOTAGE

Film-makers in the West Coast optical school are obsessed by the visual aspect of film, by the potential relationship of any one image to another and by the relationship that a few images seem to share. This relationship with the film image differs from that of almost any other group, not so much in attitude as in degree. Their obsession is probably due to the light show, an art form more highly developed on the West Coast than anywhere else: for instance, the archetypal Belson *Vortex* series, Bennie Van Meter's work at the Avalon Ballroom in San Francisco with Roger Hillyard and the work of the Single Wing Turquoise Bird, the Los Angeles group based on the studio of painter Sam Francis.

While other film-makers may be equally aware of the kinetic potential of any given movie image, the West Coast film-artists have a knack of knowing, instinctively, the best way to reveal all the rhythms it possesses. Almost any moment in any of Pat O'Neill's films would serve to illustrate this point.

Even O'Neill's first semi-documentary works, *By the Sea* (1963) and *Bump City* (1964), are dominated by his superb sense of timing. In the former, a vastly superior version of Joseph Strick's *Muscle Beach,* he worked on footage supplied by Richard Abel and constructed it so the shots become increasingly energetic as the film progresses. In the final sequence, figures on the beach are slowly abstracted (through use of a process of photo-lithography which preserves hard edges unlike normal high-contrast photography), until they become a series of vibrating primary relationships. *Bump City* is a 'city symphony' of the sixties, a very painterly and sensuous portrait of Los Angeles—beautiful close-ups of neon 'items', oversize model figures (girlies) and subliminal ads. In the dark, superimposed cars cross in two directions (silent, they look like bubbles on water). Then lush close-ups of rubbish being pushed in a dump by a bulldozer.

His best-known work *7362* (1965–7) begins as an 'absolute' film in Richter's and Ruttman's sense—pure circles of light bounce on the black screens. They establish not only the rhythm of the film but the terms in which the subsequent brilliant colour images—derived through multiple and extreme high-contrast printing from an oil pump in motion and a dancing girl—should be viewed. In four parts, the film leads to an almost sexual climax at the end, making subtle use at that moment of a strobe (plate 54).[1]

Screen (1969), like James Whitney's *Lapis* and *Yantra*, is basically an all-over dot pattern movie, but O'Neill's dots are totally random; the film was put together to be run continuously in a domestic situation as a living picture—the ultimate random colour television in effect—but the eye searches for patterns and rhythms and one cannot help but suspect that somehow O'Neill put them there.

From reports, *Runs Good* (1969–70) would appear to be both the simplest and most complex of O'Neill's works. He simply combines various levels of ordinary, almost conceptual images, slightly increasing the contrast in the printing to maintain their individual 'readability', then reveals their rhythms by the relative speeds and rapidity with which they appear. At one moment one is watching a rodeo seen through the body of a go-go girl, plus a striptease artist pumping and grinding, plus a motor boat and a plane passing through at different speeds. The fact that such apparently unrelated and potentially unprepossessing material can be aesthetically satisfying is some measure of O'Neill's kinetic mastery.

Chick Strand and Burton C. Gershfield have both worked on Pat O'Neill's optical printer, which has served as the centre of a lot of activity in Los Angeles, and both have made films that

[1] '*7362* was, by the way, prepared as a three-dimensional film, with multiple projections all round the walls and ceiling of loops of separate scenes from the main panel—now the main film. It was only shown once this way, at UCLA, while O'Neill was teaching there.' (Personal letter from Bill Moritz.)

deserve mention. Strand, who was connected with the Canyon Cinema Co-operative during its early days and knew Bruce Baillie, shares something of Baillie's spiritual quality in her best film *Anselmo*. The film is constructed around a ritual-like gift-making that takes place in an open desert. Chick gives a sousaphone to Anselmo, a Mexican peasant, and the film simply extemporizes on the associations that the act arouses, seen as a series of strangely-coloured superimpositions.

Gershfield's *Now that the Buffalo's Gone* (1967) is more formal in its structure. Gershfield sets out to 'effect the audience kinaesthetically, that is, to get at their minds through their eyes in some very physical way—so they couldn't ignore what was going on . . .' His subject was the extinction of the Indian by the image of the white man. As there were no moving pictures available of the Indians as they really lived, most of the visuals are derived from stills, which Gershfield coloured in the printing process to suggest the lives being destroyed. The white man's appearance, represented by photos of gold-rush towns, factories and the cavalry, contrasts in acid colours and an aggressive strobe is present throughout (plate 55).

Fred Drummond is one of the few non-Californians (he is British) to work in a way at all comparable to O'Neill. Drummond's *Shower Proof* (1969; plate 56) was made in anticipation of the acquisition of a 16-mm film printer at the London Film-makers' Co-op, and is basically a simple demonstration of the well known fact that printing positive to positive gives an increase in contrast in the image. But the combination of Drummond's camerawork, swinging back and forth across the naked forms of a boy and girl in a shower, and the increasing abstraction each time the sequence is repeated, gives the film a great formal strength and beauty.

The film-maker who is best known for his work with the optical printer is Scott Bartlett. Scott's film *Metanomen* (plate 57) has already been discussed in terms of its relationship with Shirley Clarke's *Bridges Go Round* (see page 136). His other films to date have been *Off/On* (1967), *A Trip to the Moon* (1968) and *Moon 69* (1969; plate 58). While many film artists have been attracted to the television image (three diverse examples being Brakhage's *Oh Life—A Woe Story: The A Test News*, Marie Menken's *Wrestling* and Jud Yalkut's *P+A—I(K)*—a tribute to Nam June Paik's television concert performance), few have exploited its graphic potential as extensively as Bartlett. Like many West Coast film-makers he had extensive experience of image control through his work in light-shows—an art form in which the ability to make creative (rather than interruptive) transitions between one configuration and the next is of supreme importance. A confidence in this ability characterizes his work. Significantly, his work process is largely a 'live' one—the basic visual 'elements' come from two sources: 16-mm high-contrast loops fed straight into television circuitry where colour is induced; and a rear screen projection of the same loops with moiré patterns, liquid slide projections, etc., recorded via a television camera. These two inputs are 'crossbred'—often superimposing the same loop from each source—to provide an immediate feedback relationship. A second camera records from a monitor, and provides a further possible layer of imagery.

The great advantage of working with video is the opportunity it offers for immediate response to the taken picture, allowing for correction and intensification during the actual process of recording. In *Off/On*, Bartlett capitalizes on the weaknesses of video too, by closing in on the flickering colour dots exaggerating the hallation effect of an overstimulated input (the equivalent of solarization, but with the 'burning' look peculiar to television). But at least part of this earlier work—the final 'animated' optically-printed section—is attempting to work in an area close to O'Neill. A pair of wobbling lines divide the screen into primary colour areas (red and blue) which rapidly alternate from positive to negative and back several times a second, the shapes superimposing and appearing almost three dimensional.

Moon 69 is a more stylistically integrated work with a rather oversimplified and blatant philosophical theme—'a space-age sermon celebrating the joys of metaphysical love'. The visuals are based on footage of an airport runway at night, man in space, highflight shots from above, descending into clouds, freefalling and so on. As in the earlier film, Bartlett duplicates and mirrors images, reverses and solarizes colour, but with a greater sensitivity than before, only subtly changing the colours and showing more concern for their overall integration. In one shot, for example, he replaces a dark area on the edge of a blue cloud, seen from above in a pale green sky, with a tonally matching area of pink and red fire—it becomes almost impressionist in its colour range.

Under a Rockefeller grant scheme, the tape studios at KQED, the local San Francisco educational television station, were made available to local artists on a number of occasions in 1967 and 1968. Both Loren Sears and Bruce Conner took advantage of the scheme. Sears' *Neuro/Aesthetics* is a collection of pieces successfully exploiting video mixing techniques in live and pre-recorded situations. The final two pieces in the collection give an indication of the range covered. In *Suzanne* a dance was taped with electronic video effects, then transferred to film and recomposed in the optical printer. 'About a dozen short scene fragments were woven, like a musical score, into four precisely executed movements.' In this state it was transmitted. *Sorcery* was structured by a single moving camera that explored the relationships of two people and a few chosen objects continuously for half an hour, a five-second-delayed playback of just-recorded material providing the only source for mixing. (In a 'normal' situation there would be at least two other cameras on set and probably a source of pre-recorded material for cross-cutting purposes.)

Conner's *Liberty Crown*, a reading by Michael McClure of his poem, simply records, in time, the film-maker's response to the immediate special effects potential of television (positive to negative, diminishing images, echoes, etc.).

The desire to re-work images is not limited to film-makers with access to professional optical printing or video-mixing equipment. David Lourie, a Los Angeles film-maker, has made one of the most beautiful re-examinations of shot footage in his *Project One* (1968; plate 59) on a home-made 8-mm optical printer—a combination of a Beaulieu camera and a Bolex projector. (He reckons a Eumig projector would have been better suited ideally.) Lourie slows down and colour separates the elements of his original film, zooming in on each frame until the movement of grain dominates the picture. The informality of his source material, a figure in a domestic interior, then outside in a landscape, enhances the unexpected, mysterious quality of the images he draws from it. One interior has exactly the feeling of a Vuillard—the frames move with a slowness that Vuillard would certainly have appreciated.

Simpler, technically, is the process of rephotographing directly from the projected image—the stop frame and variable speeds available on many cameras and projectors allowing considerable flexibility. William and Birgit Hein's *Reproductions* (see page 158) was largely made this way (with the additional use of moviescope images). David Rimmer's *Surfacing on the Thames* (1970, Canada), refilmed, with lap dissolves between each frame, is a ten-second shot of two steamers passing on the Thames. Ulrich Hertzog's *Film 2 Tiel 1* (1968; Germany) intercuts re-filmed images of an estate of blocks of flats with the original footage (plate 60). Rimmer's film is tightly structured by his technique, Hertzog's is loose and repetitive, but both insist on an acute reappraisal of the nature of film and our habitual preconceptions about it.

In Michael Stewart's *Free-Form* (1968) the film as it is seen was composed entirely in-camera, shooting off a rear projection screen. As in Lourie's movie, the visual chaos of an intimately 'seen' situation—in this case, a wild dance by a young girl—

reveals intricate patterns and rhythms in slow motion. Stewart gives tension to the piece by injecting sudden kicks of 'real' speed and time.

Ken Jacobs (see page 151) has created a feature length film *Tom Tom the Piper's Son* (1968–9) by completely re-working a ready-made, silent, less than ten-minute film of the same name dating from between 1900 and 1910. The anarchy and artificiality of this forgotten work excited Jacobs—but his treatment of it is not uncritical. He extends actions in slow motion, freezing them, repeating them, breaking them off incomplete, giving new prominence to obscure figures, revealing the ambiguities of their existence—the irony of 'staged' fear, awkwardness in their apparent ease and vice versa. Again, there are sideways reflections on the audience's anticipation—Jacobs presents his images apparently as shot, with fogged leader at the end of sequences, false starts, etc., in a refusal to submit to the viewer's 'rational' preference for clinically tidy procedure. Jacobs is creating an artwork, not cataloguing a series of permutations.

The concern with the re-working of images has its roots both in Hollywood's playful manipulation of the image in the thirties, and in the more formalistic re-contexting of familiar footage by Vertov and his colleagues in Russia a little earlier. An allied development has been the collage movie, which also stems in its basic form from Vertov, but emphasizes the Dada 'recognized' absurd moment and has one further source, Fernand Léger's *Ballet Mécanique*.

Perhaps the most amazing of recent collagists is the Italian painter/film-maker, Silvio Loffredo, who with assistance from his brother Victor, began making films in Paris about twenty years ago. His method is almost the same now as it was then. He takes his acquired footage, cuts it up and adds it to his existing collection of pieces. Then at intervals he draws from his collection, selecting a frame or two or a short strip and adding it to the pieces he has already prepared. He has made more than sixteen films in this way, but most of them are still in a state of constant flux. His 'frame' subjects are people he knows or faces that interest him, places known or places attractive to him for some reason, strips of films that contain a curious movement. His eyes are definitely those of a painter, he responds to textures in film—sometimes he 'purposely ruins' the surface of the celluloid to give it a more immediately tactile quality. His most frequently seen works are the *Court Bouillon* series (1952–62; plate 63).

In 1958 Bruce Conner made what has since become the most famous collage movie of all time—the classic *A Movie*. Most of his source film came from archives, and is a mixture of obscure and famous newsreel footage. The film begins with a play on its title: 'a movie—by Bruce Conner—a movie—the end', then cuts to a chase sequence in which the participants become increasingly absurd: cowboys and indians, firemen, a rhino, an elephant, circus cyclists (he increases the pace), sky divers, water skiers, test-car drivers, each sequence now containing an accident—audiences still find it hilarious. Then the accidents become disasters, atrocities. A suspension bridge twists and distorts and later tears itself to pieces, the Hindenburg crashes to the ground and dissolves into a mass of flames, tribesmen hack into an elephant with their knives, slide-like flash frames show a firing squad blast a man to pieces and Mussolini hanging by his feet, an atomic bomb explodes 'peacefully'. Then, in the last frightening shots a woman crouches, quivering; an otter, becoming a diver, swims through a wreck, then turns upwards towards the sun.

Conner's sequence has the same rhythmic order as Richter's *Two Pence Magic*—both make use of a completely traditional technique—montage—but divorce it from its traditional role of qualifying clause in a narrative form, making it into a film structure complete in itself. The strength of *A Movie* lies in its ability to fuse a number of seemingly totally disparate happenings into one very clear image concept—the growing disorder and chaos that underlie human aspirations.

Arthur Lipsett's *Down Memory Lane* (A National Film Board of Canada Production) also uses anonymous newsreel footage in a film-collage but arrives at a very different end product. Lipsett's collection of vacuous-looking celebrities (caught, one suspects, between the glamorous shots) and manic depressive symbolism (collapsing horse, burning man) gives an insight into a specific state of mind, rather as Dali's dream sequence in Hitchcock's *Spellbound* was intended, in total contrast to Conner's more epic statement.

In Europe, Anthony Scott from Britain (known as Scottie) and Gianfranco Barucello and Alberto Griffi (Italy) have extended the collage principle in two further directions. Scottie (like Conner, a collagist in other art forms too) takes the 'chance' factor implicit in the recognition of the absurd to its logical conclusion—making the accident of his day-to-day encounters (who he meets, where he is) provide the only criteria for the selection of his material, strenuously avoiding any suggestion of a superior aesthetic purpose. *The Longest Most Meaningless Movie* consists, therefore, of adverts, complete and incomplete sequences from feature films, out-takes, sound-only film, home-movie material and so on. Often a shot or a whole sequence will repeat *ad nauseam*, sometimes whole lengths of film appear upside down and running backwards.

In the 35-mm version (it exists in 8, 16 and 35 mm) it flips left to right to reveal the soundtrack. Only when the actual celluloid disintegrates does it become invalid. This policy of total uncritical acceptance by the artist results in a parody of standard television programming practice. By rearranging familiar material into new and often absurd relationships, the viewer's traditional dependence on continuity is rudely interrupted, and in that disturbed state, some kind of re-evaluation of the material shown (either to its advantage or to its detriment) is inevitable.

Barucello's and Griffi's *La Verifica Incerta* (1965) is a much more directly calculated assault upon the supposed logic of the structure of the narrative film. Clips from a dozen or more cinemascope movies, shown still squeezed, follow each other in a perfectly logical but completely anarchic progression. The film-makers replace the conventional sequence of shots describing a simple action (opening a window, for example) with an equal number of shots, all technically 'correct' and all dealing with the same dramatic/functional situation, but which throw the event into total confusion. The hero changes person mid-shot; camera movement reverses halfway through an action; the lighting jumps from phoney blue-filter darkness to over-exposed multi-shadowed 'daylight'; and the colour range (which throughout the movie manages to reflect every imperfection of mass-produced colour prints) cuts from all-over brown to washed-out blue-green.

The structure of the film was partly based on random selection procedures and partly on a conscious attempt to manipulate the language of film—to use Kuleshov's 'creative geography' to new ends in the creation of an anti-narrative black comedy.

After their collaboration on this film (a total of eight months' solid work), Barucello and Griffi worked separately, Barucello subsequently making a number of very direct and stylistically simple political films, almost film poems, including *Costetto a Scomparire* and *Perforce* (plate 64), both extremely subtle metaphors representing his attitude to American imperialism in Vietnam.

Returning to Conner's work, *Cosmic Ray* (1961) introduces yet another type of collage film in which the collage material is integrated with original footage in a conventional montage. All that distinguishes this technique from classical Russian montage is the rapidity and frequency with which the images appear, the basic rhythmic structure in other words. *Cosmic Ray* (often shown immediately before *A Movie* and, consequently, sometimes thought to be part of that film) intercuts and superimposes fragments of found footage with shots of a beautiful girl dancing naked to Ray Charles' *What'd I say*. The cutting pace is about four times as fast as the rhythm of the song, and in this context, the girl's dance becomes a multiple expression of life force and sexual energy.

Robert Nelson's *Confessions of a Black Mother Succuba* (1965) drew directly from *Cosmic Ray* and a great number of subsequent films have likewise emulated its associative image-bombardment (for instance, Lennie Lipton's *Cornucopia* and Giorgio Turi's *Scusate il disturbo*, both of which use television as their image source).

Collage techniques have become an essential part of the film-structuring process of many young film-makers, but increasingly their application has been in an informal context.

THE INFORMAL VISION

The major achievement of the post-war American cinema has been the development of 'personal' film-making. There had been home-movies since the late twenties, but it was only through the pioneer work of the American independent film-makers, from Watson and Webber to Deren, Anger, Markopoulos and Brakhage, that the aesthetic potential of the personal film was widely recognized. While the subject matter and many of the techniques introduced by these film-makers have since become assimilated by the commercial cinema (for instance, Kubrick's debt to Belson and the Whitneys in *2001*), there is at least one area of personal film-making which, almost by definition, must remain informal—the cinema of Robert Branaman, Abbott Meader, Alfredo Leonardi, Pia Epremian, Dore O, Klaus Schoenherr, Massimo Bacciagalupo, Takahiko Iimura and many other fine film-makers. These film-makers, whose aesthetic has its deepest roots in the emancipated home-movie of Stan Brakhage, draw directly from life, from daily vision; theirs is an extension of the eighteenth-century journal or diary—a documentary form almost—but a documentary far removed from the pre-structured, pre-concluded observations that usually go by that name. This is not to say that they are not concerned with structure, the very opposite is the case, but these film-makers believe that the material they shoot should reveal its own unique structural relationships through the process of shooting and editing. Thus, as in painting, the subject of the work is as much the process of its formation as the nature of the objects it photographically represents. They believe, with Proust, Matisse and Bonnard, that even the most routine part of daily life, the simplest act, contains significant relationships and meanings that can be revealed by repeated, patient, intuitive perceptions (both by the film-maker and his audience). The difference between this and the commercial cinema's approach to structuring is illustrated by a comment by Brakhage: 'I always found it superficially easy to edit for the commercial film industry, which isn't even concerned with the statement that a strip of film has to offer, but only with what it represents.'[1] This difference can be illustrated by taking the arbitrary example of a shot of a person going through a doorway. In a feature movie the act is a functional one, necessitated by continuity, 'he enters the room'; the 'statement' that the same strip might offer in a Brakhage movie could be an emotive movement of the person, a quality of light or an associative or kinetic relationship with the previous shots, or a combination of them all.

Even at its simplest, in its most documentary form—as in Peter Goldman's *Pestilent City* (1965)—the informal movie is capable of recording 'reality' with great emotional intensity. *Pestilent City* was made as a study for part of the feature *Echoes of Silence* and it simply establishes a number of elementary rhythms—the non-human electric pace of 42nd Street and the irregular, fumbling rhythm of the down-and-outs and unfulfilled men that people the place. Equally simple and 'documentary' is a beautiful film by John Broderick, *Tenth Street*—a record of children playing in a tiny yard, seen from several floors above. Broderick uses one basic camera position and three or four lenses to give a variety of angles—from a view of the complete yard and surrounding buildings to a relative close-up. The children's games (they were totally unaware that they were being filmed) give the film its structure and its unity—Broderick's editing-in-camera simply responds to the dynamic of their movements. It is possible to 'justify' both these films by emphasizing the 'social' record that they make, but that distorts their real position and value.

David Brooks' work, while maintaining the technical simplicity of *Pestilent City* and *Tenth Street*, demonstrates the freedom of the informal, personal film from such literal interpretation. Brooks' strips of film represent a chain of physical locations, but their statement becomes a spritual one. He describes *Winter 64–66* as: 'Door golden night room trees fire drip rain blue horse river snow birds green mountain forest dark room mist car trees window ducks are flying.' His description could equally well summarize *Nightspring Daystar* (1964) or *Letter to DH in Paris* (1966), for any inventory of his films is as meaningless as an inventory of a painting by Bonnard. It is through the lyrical flow of his camera, through his intuitive knowledge of the right length of each shot and the natural grafting of one on to another, that his statements

[1] Note from a section headed 'move meant' in *Metaphors on Vision* published by *Film Culture*, New York.

on film assume the quality of poetry. Brooks' camera moves through a landscape in a car, taking in the passing landscape in long sweeps, then watches faces in firelight, then contrasts window (blue) and lamp (orange) light. His use of sound is equally intuitive; he cuts between rock, classic and eastern music with absolute confidence.

Eel Creek (1968), one of his last films (he was killed in a car crash in early 1969), he shot with sync. sound; the addition of the spoken word and natural sounds allowed him to simplify his style even further. He (the camera) walks with a group of friends down through a field to the edge of a stream. One of them fishes; they talk among themselves and the sun sets. His acceptance of the scene is total and inspires total empathy in the viewer.

This same intensity of the informal vision distinguishes Peter Ungerleider's film of the Rolling Stones free concert in Hyde Park, *Under My Thumb* (1969), in which, in silence, he concentrates almost exclusively on the face and movements of Mick Jagger, revealing the expressionist-like dynamics of Jagger's performance. In the absence of sound, in the absence of the back and forth cutting and endless zooms that have come to typify the 'pop' film, one can at last see that Jagger is a great performer in the theatrical sense, a fact that few of his vast audience can be aware of.

Warren Sonbert was recognized as a talented film-maker while still at school; his early films reflect the social and cultural life-style that accompanied the artistic breakthrough in New York in the sixties. They are peopled by the young jet set, by super stars and their hangers on, by the opening-night crowds at the Green Gallery, at MOMA, at the Janis, but also by a crowd of slightly less sure of themselves adolescent friends. He films this world not as a statistician but as an enthusiastic participant. His films have the glamour of the Supremes, of Radio City Music Hall and Hollywood movies (he sometimes includes moments from his favourite movies by filming them off the cinema screen); his early titles reflect this love—*Where did our Love go?* (plates 70 and 71), *Hall of Mirrors*, *The Tenth Legion*, *The Tuxedo Theatre*.

Now that Sonbert is older, he is less concerned with dazzle, but his love of surfaces is still there. In his recent untitled films, the camera remains more static, more composed; he travels the world with it, comparing surfaces, placing side by side places and events from apparently opposed cultures, drawing them together into one complete whole. He establishes a basic sympathy between shots by his emphasis on colour, light and movement, that brings them together and transcends their diary content, creating a new, uniquely cinematic form.

The abandoning of the literary narrative form gave film-makers a freedom to structure their films according to the technical limits of the camera. In the case of the 'diary' film, a new form was created by the extended use of the single-frame mechanism—the device responsible for the frame-clusters in Markopoulos' work. Taylor Mead, whose *My Home Movies* (1964) and *European Diaries* (1966) were made this way, gives an off-hand description of how he came by the method:

> My home movies which weigh two pounds so far, began in Mexico City where I got bored and bought a fifty-foot Keystone at National Pawn Shop—I was immediately turned on—to the City, to Mexico—it really makes a difference—and in 16 mm—but I wanted to shoot in color and it costs about ten dollars for fifty feet in Mexico, so I had to push the single-frame button much of the time—Oh me, but it's lovely anyway—I kept on pushing once I crossed the border into US also and NY and Malibu.

The fact that two totally opposed frames side by side will superimpose when projected gives continuity a new meaning in the shooting of these movies—one has to take more than one frame of a scene for it to register on the retina. So the amount of frames shot at any one time, and the exact distance between them in terms of time and physical space (seconds, minutes, feet, miles), has great significance in the final work.

Jonas Mekas' *The Diaries* (especially the sections shown separately—*Report from Millbrook* 1966, *Hare Krishna* 1966, and *Circus Notebook* 1955; plate 73) are probably the finest of such condensed works. Jonas' great strength is that he obeys no rules, he shoots in short bursts of 'real' time and in rapid-fire single frames—stretching out certain actions within the kinetic framework of a sequence so that a figure suddenly floats serenely in the general excited field. Jimmy Tirrof's *Brigit's Dream* (1965) and Bruce Conner's *Looking for Mushrooms* (1960–6) are other beautiful examples of this emancipated technique.

Jeff Keen in Britain makes films using the diary form and collage animation, fusing the two elements together in an extraordinary graphic combination. Keen, who shot *The Autumn Feast* for Piero Heliczer in 1964, shoots both on 8 and 16 mm, his 8-mm work being mostly Mekas-like diaries of events and happenings shot collectively by whoever is present; his 16-mm works, as in *Marvo Movies* (1967/8; plate 74) and *Meatdaze* (1970), are more energetically constructed from layer upon layer of comic strip collage, time-lapse cartooning, languid reconstructions of Hollywood vamps (Keen shares Jack Smith's obsession with Mario

Montez and the great Hollywood, non-actress, star tradition) and graphic image destruction (burning plastic toys, barbed-wire-entanglement-time-lapse grafitti).

Among the younger, more recent American film-makers to follow in Stan Brakhage's footsteps are Saul Levine, James Herbert and Andrew Noren, and a brief description of one work by each of them is given here as an indication of the directions in which this genre is developing.

Saul Levine's *Note to Patti* (1968/9) concerns images of winter, children playing in snow, trees, a bird flying through branches. Every part of the film-making process is accepted by Levine as being a potential contributor to the finished look of his film—the splice marks, which appear on 8-mm films as horizontal bars about a third from the top or bottom of the frame (normally a distraction) are totally integrated in his work, giving both a 'blink-like' stimulation to vision and a positive source of movement. In certain sections they become so tactile that when the image moves within the frame it comes both as a surprise and a revelation. Levine composes with colour absolutely as an artist, taking full advantage of the saturation possible on reversal stock. The red hats of the children in the snow have the intense luminosity of a Renoir; his cutting between stocks with differing colour biases (pale pink, blue/green) gives further contrast and richness to the image.

James Herbert's *Porch Glider* (1970) is constructed round the life and activity of the front porch of a house in Athens, Georgia. The porch is first represented darkly through superimpositions of dew on ironwork, cobwebs, scenes from later in the film; then through daytime images, kids running on the grass, climbing, swinging in trees, cars passing, people walking, actions sometimes condensed so that a whole cycle appears as one. Then there are images shot through heavy rain. Halfway through, the film changes. The swinging seat on the porch (the 'glider'), where earlier the kids were playing their guitars, looking out at the world, becomes the scene for a very contained section on love-making. It is night and very open and there is a light bulb hanging just above the lovers—they are over-exposed but surrounded by darkness. Sometimes they are observed through an open window from inside the house. Sometimes the window magnifies them (Herbert replaces a pane of glass with a screen and projects the larger images on to it). The love-making is explicit and intense, but seldom reaches a climax. A brief scene of collective love-making follows before the daytime images reassert themselves. The camera is obsessive in the way it watches, and is almost unselective on occasions, but with the passion of an adolescent.

Andrew Noren's *Kodak Ghost Poems* (1970) is the most intimate and informal of the three films, its simple purpose being to record moments observed in the film-maker's life by simple comparisons: flesh and cloth, a glow, a colour, a texture, a camera-state, actions, movements, moments of intense pleasure, sex, the details of life. Any description of the feelings and associations raised by Noren's image-flow is at once totally subjective. The pattern of his images is as complex and 'irrational' as (uncensored) brain activity—and as full of the same fleeting half-recognized stimuli. Response to this film is of necessity intuitive and one only begins to appreciate the various levels involved after repeated viewing.

In the informal film, as in any other, the concentration of the image around one particular situation intensifies the experience. In Carl Linder's work a collage of quasi-surrealistic, theatrical elements is introduced into the informally photographed domestic subjects, giving each a layer of heavily Freudian associations. *The Devil is Dead* (1964) is a Bosch-like exploration of tactile sensations (combing, touching, sucking, bleeding, tearing) through overblown close-ups of limbs and organs in multiple superimposition. His treatment borders on the narrative, there being a definite pre-ordained sequence to the film and a pivotal central character, a young man 'inhabited' by this neurotic eroticism; but the emphasis is always upon the evocative quality of the images. In *Skin* (1965), flowers provide the central metaphor. Linder explores the exotic reproductive organs of flowers in lyrical camera movements, cutting in brief glimpses of their human counterparts; their vulnerability and inevitable violation being suggested by a figure (Jack Smith), seen always in the background behind the flowers, apparently defiling them.

Only a small number of film-makers in the USA are involved in making this kind of surrealist statement, but in Belgium, the traditional home of Surrealism, it is very much the dominant style, seen, for example, in three recent films: *La Ballade des Amants Maudits* (1967) by Roland Lethem, *Narcose* (1967) by Philippe Graff and *Junkies Island* (1968) by Louis Langled.

In France, Etienne O'Leary, a French Canadian, and Pierre Clementi both produced examples of informal cinema, partly under the influence of Taylor Mead's *Diaries*, partly through seeing the Jonas Mekas New American Cinema collection of films. O'Leary was first with *Day Tripper* (1965), a Dwoskin-like study of a girl smearing herself black, then becoming clean again, all while she dances; then *Homeo* (1967), a film full of superimpositions which directly inspired Clementi to turn to film-making. Clementi's best-known work is *Visa de Censure* (1967/8), an eclectic, theatrical film, again making full use of superimpositions, patterns of neon light and time-lapse photography, culminating in the image of a huge black spider crawling out of Clementi's mouth.

MINIMAL MOVES AND ANTI-AESTHETIC SEX

Though the psychodramas of Anger, Harrington and the early Brakhage never showed sexual intercourse explicitly, their direct anti-moralistic approach to sexuality made it inevitable that sexual acts would ultimately become a natural part of the subject matter of the personal film. Perhaps it was equally inevitable that it should be in the context of the informal 'diary' film that they should first appear (as in Brakhage's *An Avant-garde Home Movie*, Carolee Schneemann's *Fuses*, Noren's *Kodak Ghost Poems* and many others). But in the informal movie, love-making, though real, remained impressionistic—consciously part of an art form—and not all film-makers were content to work within that particular context.

Ken Jacobs began making films with his 'star' Jack Smith during the late fifties. Their preoccupations at that time had much in common with the contemporary 'happenings' of Alan Kaprow, Jim Dine and Claes Oldenberg, an affection for the refuse of society—both in the material and human sense in Jacobs' work. Jacobs and Smith were able to translate their work into theatrical terms; they attempted to mount a review together—*The Human Wreckage Show*—in 1961. Their first and finest film collaboration, *Blonde Cobra* (1959–62), consists of fragments of abused camera work (by Bob Fleischner) and great lengths of black leader, accompanied by a vast, rambling but inspired monologue by Smith (published complete in *Film Culture* 29). This major work introduced a new element to the American avant-garde film—a calculated technical and aesthetic decadence, a deliberate denial of the sense of boredom that severely frustrated and outraged most audiences.

Smith's own *Flaming Creatures* (1963; plate 76) has been attacked for moral decadence on more than one occasion, and became the victim of more than one court case. His subject is a transvestite orgy and the footage contains a number of shots of male genitals; yet nothing could be less likely to deprave or corrupt. The orgy ended long before the film began, years ago maybe; the 'creatures' stagger around making a last grotesque and ambiguous attempt at gang rape, then collapse in their coffins. A penis is wagged at the camera; in a tableau another appears resting on the shoulder of a creature, its owner oblivious to everything. An earthquake rouses the creatures into further zombie-like movements. The film-stock is unevenly exposed, the editing apparently minimal and arbitrary, the music nostalgic and repetitive, yet the film, not despite but because of these elements, gains an extraordinary formal integrity. The static camera allows the viewer to appreciate the Delacroix-like chance compositions that the creatures adopt, to enjoy an unexpected change of angle (the overhead shots are amazing) and the crude extended shaking of the camera that suggests the earthquake.

Flaming Creatures also established a standard of non-acting that was quickly adopted by both film directors (Ron Rice, Bill Vehr and Andy Warhol) and theatre directors (Ronald Tavel, Charles Ludlam and John Vaccaro).

Ron Rice, who died in 1964, was one of the few undisputed geniuses of the underground cinema. He completed only three works in his lifetime and a rough-cut of a fourth, each being quite separate and distinct from the others, all of them revealing the influence of other film-makers and influencing many in turn. His first film *The Flower Thief* (1960) was shot in San Francisco, starring his and Vernon Zimmerman's discovery, Taylor Mead, who became the epitome of the underground non-actor star. Rice dedicated *The Flower Thief* to the 'wild man'—the anarchic comic genius of the silent movies, but it pays equal tribute to the spirit of the Beat poets in San Francisco at that time. In *Senseless*, shot in Mexico in 1962, he acknowledges his debt to the Dada movement in a title at the beginning. Despite his scorn for conventional technique, Rice had precisely the 'eye' that Callenbach chides Brakhage for lacking (see page 131). He was incapable of taking a graceless shot, but the overall beauty of his work is a measure of his intuitive ability to put sequences together, not linked by any narrative continuity but by the wildman's inspired juxtaposition of image/ideas. Thus *Chumlum* (1964; plate 77), Rice's contribution to the transvestite orgy genre, is consciously structured by the movement between the layers of superimpositions of erotically swinging hammocks and hanging veils, which he photographed in rich colour (in strong contrast to Smith's austere black and white 'creatures').

The limbo in which these fantasies take place has proven a very potent image, and several film-makers in America and Europe have been inspired by it. In Italy, Antonio DeBernardi, a film-maker who works almost entirely in Super 8 mm, has produced a number of works including *Dei* (1968) in which similar exotic-costumed beings lounge about and amuse themselves in several layers of superimposition. In DeBernardi's film, however, the impact derives from his sense of camera rhythm and the hypnotic repetitions of the simultaneous independent soundtracks.

Bill Vehr's contributions to this kind of film, *Avocada* (USA 1965) and *Brothel* (1966), emphasize its affinities with Hollywood. His writhing woman in *Avocada* mimics the exaggerated, perverse (because of the implicit unnatural restraints of censorship) body movements of a 'movie star in torment'. *Brothel* is best described by Carl Linder: 'Gustave Moreau, piles of bodies . . . seeing parts that don't work, a Von Stroheim bordello when the cameras weren't grinding.' Vehr, like Smith, works equally in the theatre, being a member of the Vaccaro, Tavel and Ludlam Theatre of the Ridiculous Company (for whom he wrote *Whores of Babylon*, *Turds in Hell* and other choice titles). The Theatre of the Ridiculous is exactly what it calls itself, but it is an important phenomenon in the New York cultural scene none the less, as it embodies the particularly New York nostalgia for Hollywood mythology, its transexual camp and dedicated indulgence in inflated theatrical non-events. Significantly, at least half of the popularity of Andy Warhol's movies is attributable to his shrewd recognition of these same ingredients; his use of the 'Ridiculous' writer Ronald Tavel and stars Mario Montez and Jackie Curtis is not just coincidental. But Warhol had at least one highly original contribution to make —his rediscovery of the static one-shot movie (the 'actuality' of Lumière brought to life), a formal device of the first order that provided Tavel's scripts with a complementary image of equal visual integrity.

Warhol's first film, *Tarzan and Jane Regained . . . Sort of* (1963), was shot in Hollywood and was a loosely-constructed, rambling, two-hour movie in the informal style of Rice and Zimmerman, but Warhol established his static aesthetic immediately afterwards with *Sleep* (1963/4), *Eat* (1963), *Haircut* (1964), *Blow Job* (1964), *Empire* (1964) and so on. The formal statement in these silent films is everything: the confrontation of the audience with an image that changed in conventional terms only marginally and only over a long period of time; once again, audiences were outraged. It was, however, an affirmation of the principle of nonactivity and his faith in the superficial aspect of seen objects that closely parallels his silk-screen paintings. In the Tavel scripted works, *Harlot*, *Screen Test*, *The Life of Juanita Castro*, *Horse*, *Vinyl*, *Kitchen* (all 1965) and *Hedy* (*The Shopper* 1966), the action became more probing. Tavel, as a homage to Warhol, constructed his plots as a series of *tableaux vivants* but created dramatic conflict through the confrontation of the 'actors' with their script or a prearranged environment. Invariably, there is some sexual ambiguity to resolve: in *Screen Test*, Mario Montez, posing as a star auditioning for a part, is made to face the fact of his masculinity in the simplest possible (physical) way; in *Hedy* (supposedly inspired by Miss Lamarr's alleged shop-lifting court case) the star (Mario again) is confronted with the decline of her screen career and the unsatisfactory conclusion of her five marriages. But the real conflict is of the actors with their roles. Neither Tavel nor Warhol provides enough information to allow a 'routine' performance; the relentless presence of the camera demands that the actors complete the role themselves; the result is a transparent fluctuation between total absorption in the myth (role playing) and a state of very vulnerable self-revelation.

When Tavel withdrew from Warhol's movies, Warhol's reputation was already sufficient to leave him with a self-perpetuating casting system—his actors finding their own way to his studio. Increasingly the onus of the work was put on them and a group of stalwarts, his Superstars, evolved through successive movies: Nico, Gerard Malanga, Rene Ricard, Ingrid Superstar, International Velvet, Brigid Polk, Ed Hood, Pope Ondine, Taylor Mead, Louis Waldon and, most recently, Viva; each developed a personal screen personality akin to the never-changing presence of Debbie Reynolds, Cary Grant, Troy Donahue, Kim Novak (and other stars equally loved by Warhol), combined with a late-show interviewer's ability to provoke and draw out their screen partner, but revealing more than a little of themselves in the process.

In *Chelsea Girls* (a compilation of thirty-minute films from 1965–6), *My Hustler* (1966; plate 79), *I a Man* (1966), *Bike Boy* (1967) and *Lonesome Cowboys* (1967; plate 80) the dramatic conflict is basically a verbal one, a situation in which one character after another becomes the subject of interrogation about sexual and behavioural attitudes. The nudity and sexual frankness that led to their popularity with audiences is almost always quite arbitrary and unfulfilled, made even less erotic as Warhol's concern with camera movement and editing increased, by violent zoom shots and flash-frame jump-cuts in picture and soundtrack. As the structural story line diminished, the subtlety of the situations increased in proportion. From ****, the twenty-four-hour movie (1968), through the *Imitation of Christ* (drawn from the twenty-four-hour work), *Nude Restaurant* (1968) to *Fuck* (alternatively called *Blue Movie* or *Louis and Viva*, 1969), the confrontations have become increasingly less schematic—in *Fuck*, Louis Waldon and Viva simply talk together, fry eggs, wash and make love, still playing the mental games of sophisticated city-folk but showing for the first time a genuine sense of respect and affection. This is perhaps the first genuine narrative-film love story; it is also the first film in which Warhol shows a sexual act in its entirety. That he should choose this film in which to do it, while his assistant/manager Paul Morrissey expediently veers towards Hollywood's prurient self-censorship in his D'Allesandro vehicles *Flesh* (1968) and *Trash* (1970), is hopefully a sign of Warhol's continued aesthetic integrity.

In 1969 Stan Brakhage announced his new work *Lovemaking*, a film in four parts containing absolutely explicit scenes of lovemaking between men and women, men and men, and children in ritual erotic stimulation. His professed intention was to 'do for the blue movie what he had already done for the home-movie' (through his 8-mm work). He was stating, in effect, his determination to elevate the subject of pornography to an art form, an ambition almost totally contrary to that of the Austrian filmmaker, Valie Export, who believes that any representation of sex on the screen is dangerous and an evasion of the central issue, and should be replaced by a direct confrontation with the 'real'. Her piece *Tapp und Tastfilm* (plate 81) challenges the 'spectator' to touch the object that so fascinates him when it appears naked or partly unclothed on the silver screen.

A more Brechtian view is taken by Rosa von Praunheim (Germany) whose films are dedicated to the emancipation of women and the fight for complete social freedom for the male homosexual. His movies mix winning soap-opera acting and romantic music with slogans and tract reading in an attempt to assault the masses through an aesthetic they are familiar with.

By far the most influential statements being made in Europe on the subject of sex are those centred on the work of Herman Nitsch and Otto Muehl. The 'materialaktions' of Muehl have been the subject of films by Kurt Kren, Peter Weibel, Ernst Schmidt as well as Muehl himself. They have developed since they were first recorded on film in 1964 from emphatically tactile happenings involving their naked participants with paint, food, plants, feathers, etc., to an all-out attack upon the audience's sexual sensibilities. Muehl has no time for film aesthetics, his films are not always well made and are becoming stylistically repetitive, but this means nothing to him. *Sodoma* (1969) is a recent compilation of earlier 'materialaktions', where the participants perform every conceivable outrage upon each other, killing animals and inflicting severe pain in an orgy of tortures, destructive anally-obsessed sex. The theory is one of catharsis—expiation almost—a purging of collective sexual guilt. Though Vienna is the home of Muehl, his films cannot be shown there but he has found a regular and profitable outlet for his films in Germany.

The best argument for this position is made by Kurt Kren, who manages through his masterly editing and sense of rhythm to convey something of a sense of humour in his film records. His positive attitude is best illustrated by an original subject of his own *16/67 20 September* (*The Eating Drinking Pissing Shitting Film*), a brilliant kinetic working of these actions (seen in close-up) into one vital (life-enhancing) mental image—a task that few film-makers would undertake and even fewer could successfully achieve.

STRUCTURAL CINEMA

P. Adams Sitney has devised the term 'structural cinema' to describe the development of a new aesthetic movement away from the increasing complexity-consciousness of, for instance, Brakhage, Markopoulos and Anger, towards a more formal determination of subject and technique. The achievements of Richter and Léger had suggested two lines of development: one towards kinetic studies (abstract animation and single-frame photography) as in the elemental play of light (moving squares) in Richter's *Rhythmus 21*; another towards the recognition of the physical properties of film—the 'film as the (only) subject of film' school (as in the lady climbing stairs in Léger's *Ballet Mécanique*).

In the fifties, Robert Breer and Norman McLaren made important contributions to kinetic studies: McLaren with his *Blinkety Blank* (1955), in which his obsessional hen, egg and floating shapes appear at first only intermittently (from one frame in ten), then in bursts of complete animation (one in every four), in what he described as a demonstration of the eye's ability to retain an image until it is replaced by another. Breer made *Recreation* (1956), a 'frame by frame collision of totally disparate images', *Jamestown Baloos* (1957), a mixture of collage animation and actual scenes, and *Blazes* (1961), 'a hundred basic images switching positions for four thousand frames'.

One of Breer's discoveries was the simple fact that two different images on consecutive frames give the effect of a single superimposition; the chain of different images means the eye has to choose what it wants to see. A large number of films have been produced exploiting this effect: William and Birgit Hein's *S+W* (1967 Germany), Victor and Silvio Loffredo's *Court Bouillon* series, Guido Lombardi's alternate-frame *Sviluppo Number 2* (1968), the work of collagists Bruce Conner and Jeff Keen, and the diaries of Taylor Mead and Jonas Mekas. However, with the exception of the Heins, these film-makers made conscious attempts to include recognizable emotional or associative references in their work, thus excluding them from the 'structural' frame of reference, although the kinetic quality of their work remains essential to their meaning.

The first major frame-by-frame kinetic abstraction in recent years was Peter Kubelka's *Arnulf Rainer* (1957, Austria), a meticulously-composed work consisting of single and grouped black-and-white frames, counterpointed with black-and-white sound—the premise of Richter's *Rhythmus* series taken to its ultimate conclusion. Kubelka is one of the most fastidious film-makers—his films totalling thirty-four minutes have taken him fifteen years to make. In *Adebar* (1956/7), the movement of dancing figures is reduced to a rhythmic, jerky black-and-white silhouette, alternating in positive and negative and repeating hypnotically. It lasts for one minute. In *Schwechater* (1957/8) a glimpse of people drinking in a café is treated in a similar way, the film becoming an aesthetic composition of the movement of objects in light. *Arnulf Rainer* and *Schwechater* owe as much to Léger as to Richter—the division between the sensibilities is by no means rigid.

Unsere Afrikareise (1961–6), Kubelka's most recent work, transcends all classification; it is a masterly piece of editing, picture and sound editing—they are equally important and complement each other as in no other film. As a record of a trip to Africa it is quite unspectacular and the images are cut with a precision that emphasizes their simplicity and 'naturalness'; yet his technique reveals their meaning with the exactitude of the most calculated 'artificial' Russian montage. Kubelka has proved that by learning every frame and every sound by heart before editing, one can produce a totally unambiguous work.

Kurt Kren (Austria) has been making films since 1957. His work falls into two categories: his single-frame records of Otto Muehl's happenings (see page 154) and his experiments in cinematic form. One facet of his happening films should be mentioned here, his use of splice marks (as in *7/64 Leda and the Swan*). Kren was the first film-maker after Brakhage to make creative use of the horizontal bar caused by splices—they become an integral part of the visual rhythm of the picture.

Kren's ability to create a kinetic drama out of repeated (sometimes re-edited) loops is equal to that of Kubelka in *Adebar* and *Schwechater*. *2/60 Faces from the Szondi Test* was an introductory work, in which faces taken from coarsely-printed illustrations (of criminal types?) are shown one frame each in different sequences. The result is a single, rhythmically evolving face, the areas of movement being around the mouth, eyes, neck, etc.

In *4/60 Walls Positive Negative*, he presents his images in a rapid montage, the pace quickening with each repetition (the title describes it).

In *15/67 TV* (1967; plate 90) Kren's subject is a simple view of a lakeside from a window: a girl sits on a bollard, sometimes swinging her leg, another passes by on roller-skates, a crane starts to cross the window; inside a silhouette of a face begins to obscure the view. Kren establishes a basic loop rhythm which he repeats twenty-one times, marking each revolution with black leader. Then by (magical) editing he manages to make every movement unexpected, yet quite undramatic. It is a masterpiece. I have seen it maybe a dozen times and still cannot see what he does—perhaps there is no editing at all.

In America, some of the first film-artists to consciously enter the field of Structural Cinema belonged to the Fluxus group. In 1966 they put together a collective reel that included a number of single-frame and single-take films, including Paul Sharits' *Wrist Trick*, *Dots* and *Sears Catalogue*, Yoko Ono's first bottoms film *Number 4* (a twelve-minute version), *Entrance-Exit* by George Brecht—a simple progression of frames from black through to white—and the anonymous *Ten Feet*, a stretch of film calibrated as a measuring tape (an archetypal structural film if ever there was one) lasting seventeen seconds.

In the same year, Tony Conrad made *The Flicker*, 'the first fully atmospheric development of stroboscopic light as an expressive medium'. Conrad's premise is more conceptual than Kubelka's; it is perhaps even a regression in that his achievement is much closer to the minimal stand taken by Warhol and others. His flicker is a simple progression from twenty-four flashes per second (camera speed) to four flashes and back to twenty-four in the space of thirty minutes.

Paul Sharits, on the other hand, has developed the flicker principle to include colour frames, in sequences fiercely structured to remove all emotional association, evenly paced single frames of images, photographed against plain backgrounds (almost like some fashion photographs) to reduce them to a conceptual level.

Ray Gun Virus (1966) contains no figurative images and comes close to being an attack upon the (pre-) conceptual nervous system of the viewer, but Sharits asserts its thematic structure: 'The sense of striving, leading to mental suicide and death, and then rhythms of rebirth.' In *Peace Mandala/End War* (1967; plate 94) and films made since, the theme becomes the responsibility of the colour changes, the images being introduced as subjects for meditation almost, hence their detachment from a 'natural' environment. In *Peace Mandala*, a naked couple are seen alternately from either side, in different phases of making love; in the central portion of the film, the film-maker is seen with a gun to his head, an animated line indicating the path of the bullet. In *N:O:T:H:I:N:G:* a chair is falling backwards, a light bulb ingesting animated beams of light, shining black, melting. No other film-maker has managed to present figurative images in such an affirmative, yet association-free way.

George Landow's films are the apotheosis of the 'film as film' aesthetic. Like many others working in this field, Landow's approach to the film image reflects his background as a painter:

> In painting you start with a blank canvas, you start with nothing and you create your image particle by particle; whereas in film, usually you just open your lens and you have a vast quantity of objects which become part of your image.

Landow's *Fleming Falcon* (1963) serves as an introduction to his material—a multiplicity of taken images cramming the screen with as many as ten distinct frames at a time. In *Film in which there appear Sprocket Holes, Edge Lettering, Dirt Particles, etc.* (1965–6), the material is reduced to a minimum: a lab colour test-strip of a girl's head and colour bars appear twice in the height of the projected frame and one-and-a-half times in the width. The half-image of the girl on the right-hand side rapidly blinks her one visible eye—which is right against the edge of the frame—providing (together with the self-superimposition of the edge lettering) all the 'real' movement in the picture. The strip has been loop printed in exact repetition, the only difference being in the accumulation of dust particles in the row of sprocket holes visible in the centre of the picture.

In *Bardo Follies* (1967; plates 91 and 92), Landow moves towards the spiritual position of Sharits, the structural progression of the images 'paraphrasing certain sections of the *Bardo Thodol*', the *Tibetan Book of the Dead*. The film begins with a looped image of a girl waving to a passing fairground boat. The same loop then becomes two, then three smaller images set in a black field; then each circle freezes and burns in succession; then the whole screen burns (the celluloid apparently blistering and flaking off), the rhythmic structure of the loop still being maintained by repetition. In the final sequences, the screen divides and bubbles form on either side, echoing the blisters and the circular shapes of the multi-images, but replacing the loop with their own boiling rhythm. The film stops quite suddenly. The progress is from the extravagant artificial image to the play of pure light; from a rigid repeat mechanism, to an evolving, living one. In *The Film that rises to the Surface of Clarified Butter* (1968), Landow takes the situation of the cartoonist's trick of 'bringing drawings to life' in the presence of their author and by looping it, forces an acknowledgment of the equal illusory nature of both 'realities'. His materials are two sets of front and back shots of the animator, the drawings (of a grotesque human shape) and a girl pointing at them. As if it were inevitable, the events take on a reality of their own and become fixed in the mind as a complete event in themselves.

The work of Landow reveals a wealth of material that other film-makers have dealt with in part and sometimes in more specific detail. Bruce Conner's use of the loop in *Report* (1965), his film on the death of Kennedy, is no less formal than Landow's, but highly emotive. It opens with stock shots of the Kennedys 'on tour' intercut with shots of Jackie after the assassination and the funeral procession. Thus the morbid 'suspense' of a sequential presentation is destroyed. Then, Conner introduces the loops: first a chain of policemen passing a gun (Oswald's?) down a line of hands. The looping makes an 'innocent' activity into a fascist threat. Then there is a shot of the Presidential car coming round a corner among thick crowds just before the shooting. The shot does not appear. Each time round the loop starts and finishes a little further through the movement. The image is a cheerful one, the pressing forward of the crowd quite 'normal', but the feeling of foreboding is ominous. The soundtrack is a continuous replay of a radio commentary recorded at the time. When the shot is announced the images break into an extended coda of newsreels, television advertisements, a bullfight, etc., providing one of Conner's most caustic observations on the American mind.

Closer to Landow's aesceticism are Malcolm Le Grice (Britain) and William and Birgit Hein (Germany). Both have made variants upon the theme of *Films in which there appear Sprocket Holes* . . . Le Grice's *Little Dog For Roger* is an almost lyrical two-screen treatment of repeating sections of 9·5 mm home-movie footage in positive and negative, superimpositions, etc., showing his mother and her dog out walking; the Heins' *Grün*, *Rohfilm* (plate 93) and *Reproductions* include actual film collage and hand attacks upon the celluloid as well as wandering frame-lines and sprocket holes. Although the Heins' technique in these films is less structural, their affirmation (particularly in *Rohfilm*) of the film's substance and its physical presence in the projector is overwhelming, more powerful than any American film I have seen.

This rawness also characterizes Malcolm Le Grice's first film, *Castle 1* (*The Light-Bulb Film* 1966). The main body of the film consists of about twenty-five sections of 'found' industrial documentaries, aggressively cut without any apparent order. It opens and closes with the filmed image of a flashing light-bulb which slowly gives way to the other material, then finally re-asserts itself. But the main structure of the film is given by a real light-bulb hanging beside the screen which flashes brilliantly at regular intervals throughout, obliterating the image and forcibly reminding the audience of their surroundings.

Castle 2 (1968; plate 95), a two-screen film, uses the same kind of taken imagery (industrial/military) but in a more composed form, the film opening with a long section of sound only, then building up to an involved counterpoint between four sections of the screen—the elements of black and white being predominant. *Blind White Duration* (1968) has affinities with *Gammelion* though Le Grice had not seen any of Markopoulos' films at the time. *Blind White Duration* is purely visual (avoiding Markopoulos' narrative associations)—a subway station is seen under snow, the images appear singly or in clusters, fading in and out of white leader, static and evenly spaced.

In *Spot the Microdot, or How to Screw the CIA Part 1* (1970)—a constructed film in the sense that no processing was involved—Le Grice inserted parts of images into holes punched in magnetically-coated 16 mm film (sound tape), used because of its density, arranging them at mathematically-predicted intervals. The colours of the dots (landscape images) give a clue to the structure. The sound was created in the same way.

Ernst Schmidt, the Austrian film-maker, has made an interesting variation of this film (without knowing of its existence!) in *Weiss*, a virtually unprojectable film of white holes punched in clear leader. He was delighted to discover that the scratch marks it accumulated continue across the holes when projected, the ultimate proof of the persistence of vision.

In the Heins' more recent films the visual attack of *Rohfilm* has given way to a more studied analytical approach, in which structure plays an increasingly important role. In *625* (1969) a flickering pictureless television screen was filmed at 8, 12, 16, 24, 32 and 64 frames per second, and the resulting images appear in negative in short bursts cut in a random sequence. A new element arrives, the bar line (caused by the camera and television scan being out of phase), which varied in width and movement (up or down) according to the film speed. The flicker is, therefore, a photographable phenomenon unviewable by the human eye: the first creative use of the camera shutter in effect.

The Heins' latest film *Work in Progress Teil A* (1969-70) is a six-part film. The first part, *Takes*, shows twelve takes of the same shot from an Italian documentary—a simple statement about cinematic reality. Part two, *Catania*, is basically a three-second sequence of single-frame shots of the Bay of Catania. It was printed as single still photographs which were then re-photographed individually on an animation rostrum where a lateral 'shift' takes place; then the new film was printed as a series of 180 equal-length contact strips with differing light exposures, and again a slight shift. The resultant image when projected is technically perfectly clear, yet impossible to focus on. Part three (untitled) is a regular flicker—three frames of black and three images of two girls shown alternately for ten minutes (plate 96). Spectators report changes in pace, focus, movement in the figures, etc. Part four (untitled) is an actuality, a street scene uninterrupted, a relief after part three, 'then disgust . . . it's like going out into a street after a Western'. In part five, *The Jewellery Robbery*, fifteen images from a series of thirty-three of an actual robbery, taken by a time-lapse camera, are shown spaced out by five-second pieces of black leader. Taken from magazine illustrations, the official text is read out beforehand to remove all suspense; yet though the event is witnessed, it seems quite unreal and fails to conform to conceptual reality. Part six (untitled) repeats the technique of part two, with the addition of black and white spacing frames in sequences of one to fifteen. Three shots (33, 43 and 44 frames) of William Hein running across a room provide the subject, their continuity being totally destroyed by their context.

The choice of the title *Reproductions* for one of their earlier films was an apt one, for the Heins' films attempt to reveal just what happens in the process of reproduction—the removing of one image from another. The structure of their films, and the commonplace look of the images, frees them from association and abstraction which would tend to obscure this process of observation. They use these formal tools to achieve a freedom equivalent to Brakhage's freedom with informal techniques.

Joyce Wieland (Canada/USA) made *1933* (1967) one of her most structural films, from the same raw materials as Kren's *TV*—the view from a window. Through its bars a street is seen, cars go by, a few people walk on the far side of the road. There is something uneven about the pace of their movement (it could be natural). The single shot is repeated about a dozen times with leader, which does not always look the same, marking each repetition. The title *1933* is occasionally superimposed during the sequences. The superimposition of this formal device and the variation of the leader gives her exact repetitions the same elusive quality as Kren's *TV* which is edited.

In her *Sailboat* (1967) a single boat crosses the field of vision from left to right, a man runs down the shore in the foreground; the moment the boat completes its transit, the loop repeats, another boat sails . . . an optical game (far superior to Duchamp's academic exercise). In *La Raison avant la Passion* (1969; plate 98), her latest feature-length work, the structural elements are subordinate to an ironical purpose. The images are those of a coast-to-coast trip across Canada, their order selected by a computer; a central section interrupts the flow with an extended exposure of the 'official' face of Pierre Trudeau (accompanied by a rudimentary French lesson on the track!).

Ken Jacobs' *Soft Rain* (1969) is another 'view from the window' loop film and probably the most formal of them all. The view is seen through a gap between two buildings; a corrugated roof is below in the foreground; cars slowly pass the gap; above a certain level the view between the buildings is obscured by a black matte, which is slightly ambiguous, for on first viewing it could just be the roof of a one-storey building on the far side of the street. The take runs for one camera-reel, about three minutes (the cars go slowly by, often stopping), and only repeats three times. The matte makes an aesthetic statement out of an actuality by acknowledging the presence and judgment of the artist. It is an astonishingly poetic work.

Werner Nekes' work moves between the elliptical cutting of Kubelka and Kren, and the static one-shot film popularized by Warhol. Nekes' *Bogen* (1967), a one-minute play on human action, owes much to *Schwechater*, but in *Schnitte für ABABA* (1967) he produced a mature and completely original work. Announced as a political film, the shots of English policemen printed alternately in red and green, are cut specifically so that the splices become visible, not as an aesthetic device as in Kren or Brakhage, but as a crude announcement that 'this is a splice'.

Gurtrug 1 and *Gurtrug 2* (also 1957) are outstanding. In the former, people are seen in extreme long shot moving about in a field, their curious progress around its perimeter never seeming quite random, yet never revealing any order. The editing again seems to obey a pattern that eludes the viewer, re-emphasizing the element of doubt. In *Gurtrug 2* the whole dynamic of the screen-shape is altered; two projectors throw the same triangular image on to the screen, one inverted above the other, meeting at their apexes. As the basic image (of people lying on the floor, moving over each other) was shot from directly above, neither image is upside down. They mirror each other, the base line of each apex appearing slightly further away than their points. The film starts and stops quite arbitrarily, we are just given an opportunity to enjoy the formal composition (like a painting by Noland or Stella), or to make visual comparisons, that is all.

The Warhol one-shot film has given rise to a vast number of static films, particularly in Europe where the idea of them arrived long before the actual movies (in fact, most of the archetypal one-shots, *Eat*, *Sleep*, *Empire*, etc., still have not arrived). For instance, Lutz Mommartz's *Eisenbahn* (1967; plate 97), a fifteen-minute train ride, and Gerd Conradt's *Frederic Rzewski isst bei Carlone—Via della Luce 55—Rom Italien—26 August* (1967), a man eating spaghetti, as well as Gottfried Schlemmer's *8h01–8h11*, a record of a clock face that somehow manages to last eleven minutes—all owe their existence to Warhol. In England, Mike Dunford's 8-mm *C Movie* (1968), a gradual transformation of a paint-can on a window ledge into the waves on the seashore, is one of the few that goes beyond the basic premise to create a positive transcendental image. In the same direction, John Lennon and Yoko Ono have made several attempts to create a spiritual image in film—an image for peace. *Smile* (1968), a single extreme slow-motion shot of John's face, is an extension of an earlier Fluxus idea; but *Apotheosis* (1969), a single-take, sync.-sound ascent of the camera from ground level (with the film-makers in the foreground) to high above the clouds, works brilliantly as a purely visual metaphor of the ascending spirit.

Albie Thoms' *Bolero* (1967; plate 99), a tracking shot down the length of an Australian back street, was completed in one take but is in fact more of a study of the subjective camera (its movements relating to Ravel's music) than of structural form. However, his recent feature *Marinetti* (1968) interestingly combines a very tight control of images (appearing initially in single frames and short bursts, then gradually increasing in number until the full sequence is established) with informal diary subject matter and fantasy material.

But by far the most interesting and complex of all 'one-shot' structural films is Mike Snow's *Wavelength* (1967). In fact, neither *Wavelength*, nor his most recent full-length work ↔ (1969), are single takes in the strictest sense of the word, yet the term editing would imply dramatic action disturbed by technique, and in Snow's films exactly the opposite is the case—human action interrupts (measures) the technique.

The subject of *Wavelength* is a single zoom shot taken from a fixed position, which progresses down the length of an eighty-foot loft towards the windows at the far end. The shot takes forty-five minutes to reach its maximum extension, by which time it is focusing on a small section of a photograph pinned to the wall between two windows. The soundtrack parallels this movement with an ascending, almost deafening sine wave, starting at fifty cycles per second and ending at around 12,000. During the shot several changes of stock are made (the colour balance changes), filters are added, the exposure changes (one can see outside/one cannot see outside), one also becomes aware of imperfections, a slight change of angle, a 'jolt' in the movement of the zoom lens. Thus, though the field of vision is becoming ever more limited, one gets to know a lot about the space. Then there are the human interruptions: a bookcase is moved in and two girls listen to the radio; later a man staggers in (off) and collapses briefly passing through the picture; even later, a girl comes in, discovers the body and makes a phone call. In each case it is the cutting-out of the sine wave and its replacement by sync. sound that causes the most shock. In an early review of the film, I equated the 'freshness' of these bursts of sound to the impact of the first talkie; I still get that feeling (it is like David Brook's enjoyment of sync. sound in *Eel Creek*)—yet in Snow's film the illusion is not exactly one of 'reality'. The man collapsing, the report of his death by telephone (the dramatic ingredients of every Hollywood film ever made) are totally unmoving. The ambiguity of the reality illusion has never been so powerfully presented. But this is not the subject of the film. The subject is the real reality of the zoom shot—a reality which leads to the conclusion that the entire tonal/chromatic/ spatial experience of the room can be summarized in a single, static, black-and-white photo of a wave.

In ←→ (plate 100) Snow uses his structural device—the fixed camera's pans back and forth within a prescribed angle—to make a less philosophical but no less rewarding observation. The camera is located in a classroom; at first a number of human incidents, all apparently incidental, the rate of the camera's movement varying in relation to them. After the mid-point of the film, the human activity ends and the camera-pans rapidly increase in speed until the room is seen in purely kinetic terms, a two-dimensional movement of light on the screen. At its top speed, the direction changes to vertical and the camera movements then slow down and eventually stop. After the credits have appeared the entire film is repeated in condensed form, not in its original order, and in multiple superimposition, the various units of time measurement imposed by the panning fusing into an atemporal observation of relative movement.

Snow, himself a painter and sculptor still very active in those fields (he represented Canada in the 1970 Venice Biennale), has totally invalidated the objection raised by artists that film cannot deal with the problem of the plastic arts; and equally demolished the film-makers' belief (largely justified in the past) that graphic artists are incapable of exploiting the basic emotive power of film—the recording of the time/movement continuum.

Bibliography

Books

Bardèche, Maurice and Robert Brasillach *Histoire du Cinéma*. Paris: Les Editions Denoël et Steele 1935

Brownlow, Kevin *The Parade's Gone By*. London: Secker & Warburg 1969; New York: Alfred A. Knopf Inc. 1969

Cocteau, Jean *The Blood of a Poet* with *The Testament of Orpheus*. London: Calder & Boyars Ltd 1970

Deren, Maya *An Anagram of Ideas of Art Form and Film*. New York: Alicat Bookshop Press 1946

Durgnat, Raymond *Luis Buñuel*. London: Studio Vista 1967; University of California Press 1968

Eisenstein, Sergei M. *The Film Sense*, translated and edited by Jay Leyda. London: Faber and Faber 1963. Reissued as *Film Essays and a Lecture*. New York: Praeger 1970

Eisner, Lotte *The Haunted Screen*. London: Thames and Hudson 1969; University of California Press 1969

Fielding, R. (ed) *A Technological History of Motion Pictures and Television*. Cambridge University Press 1968; University of California Press 1968

Geduld, Harry M. *Film Makers on Film Making*. London: Penguin Books 1967; Indiana University Press 1967 (especially Dziga Vertov's '"Kinoks Reovlution", Selections')

Goodman, Ezra *The Fifty Year Decline and Fall of Hollywood*. New York: Simon and Schuster 1961

Howard, Brice *Videospace*. San Francisco: KQED 1969

Hughes, Robert (ed) *Film: Book 1*. London: John Calder Ltd 1959; New York: Grove Press 1959

Jacobs, Lewis *The Rise of the American Film*. New York: Harcourt Brace & Co 1939

Kracauer, Siegfried *From Caligari to Hitler*. Princeton University Press 1969; Oxford University Press 1969

Lapierre, Marcel (ed) *Anthologie du Cinéma*. Paris: La Nouvelle Edition 1946

Leprohon, Pierre *Le Cinéma Italien*. Paris: Seghers 1966

Lo Duca, Giuseppe Mana *Le Dessin Animé*. Paris: Prisma 1948

Loffredo, Victor and Silvio *Le Court Bouillon*. Florence: Edizioni Pananti 1970 (films collage di Victor e Silvio Loffredo)

Mancia, Adrienne and Willard Van Dyke *The Artist as Film-maker: Len Lye*. New York: Museum of Modern Art 1966

Nadeau, Maurice *The History of Surrealism*. New York: Macmillan 1965; London: Jonathan Cape 1968

Renan, Sheldon *The Underground Film.* New York: E. P. Dutton & Co. 1967; London: Studio Vista 1968

Richter, Hans *Dada, Art and Anti-Art.* London: Thames and Hudson 1965; New York: McGraw-Hill 1965

Sadoul, Georges *Histoire du Cinema.* Paris: Librairie Flammarion 1962

Sitney, P. Adams *The Reader.* New York: Praeger 1970

Stauffacher, Frank (ed) *Art in Cinema.* San Francisco: San Francisco Museum of Art 1947 (especially articles by Douglas Crockwell; John and James Whitney 'Audio-visual music')

Stephenson, Ralph *Animation in the Cinema.* New York: A. S. Barnes 1967; London: Zwemmer 1967

Youngblood, Gene *Expanded Cinema.* New York: E. P. Dutton & Co. 1970; London: Studio Vista 1971.

Periodicals

After Image (London) no.1 1969 articles on Dziga Vertov; no.2 1970 articles by P. Adams Sitney

Arts Canada (Toronto) no.142/3 1970 Gene Youngblood 'The new Canadian cinema: images from the age of paradox'

American Cinematographer (Los Angeles) 1934 Karl Freund 'What is montage'; 1936 Lynn Dunn 'Optical printing and techniques', R. W. Winton 'The Amateur Cinema League'

Canyon Cinemanews (Berkeley, California) newsletter of the Canyon Cinema Co-op

Cinema 60/61 (Paris) nos.50–2 1960–1 André Brunelin 'Au temps du Vieux Colombier de Jean Tedesco'

Cinema (Cambridge, England) no.4 1969 Tony Ryans '*Lucifer*—a Kenneth Anger Kompendium'

Cinim (London) magazine of the London Film-makers' Co-operative

Film Culture (New York) founded in 1955 by Jonas Mekas: no.19 Slavko Vorkapich 'Towards a true cinema'; no.25 'The writings of Dziga Vertov'; no.29 Maya Deren 'The Cleveland Lecture', Michael McClure '*Dog Star Man* – the first 16-mm epic; no.30 Stan Brakhage 'Metaphors on vision' (collected and edited by P. Adams Sitney); no.32 Douglas Crockwell 'A background to free animation'; no.41 Toby Mussman 'Early surrealist expression in the cinema'; no.48 Alexandre Alexeieff 'The synthesis of artificial movements in motion picture projection'

Film Quarterly (Berkeley, California) spring 1961 Ernest Callenbach's review of five Brakhage films; spring 1968 Ernest Callenbach '*Phenomena* and *Samadhi*' (on Jordan Belson), Richard Whitehall '*Now that the Buffalo's Gone*' (on Berton Gershfield); summer 1968 Jud Yalkut '*Wavelength*' (on Mike Snow)

Films in Review (New York) April 1960 Jack Spears 'Robert Florey'

Image et Son (Paris) no.207 1967 Hubert Arnault 'Cinéastes Français d'animation' (on Alexandre Alexeieff); no.224 1969 Alexandre Alexeieff and Clair Parker 'Berthold Bartosch'

Los Angeles Free Press articles by Gene Youngblood

Penguin Film Review (London) no.5 1948 Jacques Brunius 'Rise and decline of an avant-garde'; no. 9 1948 Hans Richter 'Experiments with celluloid'

Premier Plan (Paris) nos.22–4 (in one volume) 1962 entire issue devoted to Jean Renoir

Show (Los Angeles) vol.1 no.1 1970 Lita Eliscu 'Jordan Belson makes movies'

Sight and Sound (London) vol.16 no.64 1947 Alberto Cavalcanti 'Presenting Len Lye'; vol.38 no.3 1969 Alain Resnais 'Interview with Richard Roud'

Supervisuel (Zurich) European experimental magazine

Take One (Montreal) September/October 1969 Stan Vanderbeek 'Movies . . . disposable art . . . synthetic media . . . and artificial intelligence'

Tulane Drama Review (New Orleans) no.33 1966 Stan Vanderbeek 'Culture: Intercom', Antonin Artaud 'Scenarios and arguments' (especially *The Revolt of the Butcher*)

Village Voice (New York) Jonas Mekas' weekly column, Movie Journal

Miscellaneous

Lagerkatalog 1969 Progressive Art Productions, Munich 1969

Programme of the 4th International Experimental Film Competition, Cinémathèque Royale de Belgique 1967/8

TV as a creative medium, Howard Wise Gallery New York 1969

Index

Numbers in italics refer to illustration plates